Reproductive uncertainty

Understanding the regulations on assisted reproductive technologies in China

Tiantian Chen

University of Cambridge

Critical Perspectives on Social Science

VERNON PRESS

www.vernonpress.com

In the Americas:
Vernon Press
1000 N West Street, Suite 1200
Wilmington, Delaware, 19801
United States

In the rest of the world:
Vernon Press
C/Sancti Espiritu 17,
Malaga, 29006
Spain

Critical Perspectives on Social Science

Library of Congress Control Number: 2024946018

ISBN: 979-8-8819-0107-3

Also available: 978-1-64889-126-7 [Hardback]; 979-8-8819-0098-4 [PDF, E-Book]

Table of contents

Acknowledgment

Writing this book would not have been possible without the support and guidance that I received from many people. I would like to first say a very big thank you to my PhD supervisor, Professor Sarah Franklin, for all the support and encouragement she gave me. She accepted my bold PhD proposal in the first instance. Otherwise, I would not have had the courage to embark on this journey. She convinced me during many supervisions in Cambridge that my research project was achievable and meaningful. She encouraged me to turn my PhD thesis into a book. She kept a sense of humor when I had lost mine. Indeed, Sarah cared so much about my work and responded to my questions very promptly. When I came up with new ideas, she was more excited than me. She also raised many hard questions, which inspired me to widen my research from studying egg freezing as a reproductive technology to using egg freezing as a lens for broader social changes in China. In addition, she organized many seminars, such as Changing Infertilities and Remaking Reproduction that allowed me to connect with outstanding scholars in relevant fields. Sarah really gave me the fire to move forward.

My thanks also go out to Dr Lucy van de Wiel and Dr. Janelle Lamoreaux. As I was quite new to reproductive technologies at the beginning of the research project, Janelle provided me with a list of reference books at the beginning of my research. These books helped me familiarize myself with the "language" and the scholarly debates in reproduction studies. I was very grateful that Lucy provided me with detailed feedback about this book. Her feedback helped me develop and clarify my arguments. And her advice on how to think and write academically was invaluable.

Many thanks for the support I received from ReproSoc. This solid academic community often felt like a family. My colleagues, who were committed to respect, gentleness, intellectual humility, and good humor, were always so helpful throughout my research. They gave me candid advice about my research during Brown Bag Lunch, ReproSess, and academic presentations. I was delighted to be part of this community. I could still remember the sensational displays at the London Fertility Show and our struggles of approaching "fertility shoppers." I miss Dolly the Sheep's songs very much.

I gratefully acknowledge the funding received for my research from the Chinese Scholarship Council. I was also supported by the Chinese Students Award. These scholarships gave me the freedom to fully concentrate on the demanding work of my studies.

To my participants, thank you for sharing your life stories with me and for your friendship. I cannot express how open and honest all of my informants were. Though their names could not be disclosed, I want to appreciate their help and transparency during my fieldwork.

I would also like to say a heartfelt thank you to my Mum and Dad for always encouraging me to bravely pursue my research ideas. Thanks to my relatives and friends for contacting gatekeepers at clinics and organizations, finding informants, and offering me advice. They helped me in whatever way they could during the challenging four years. A very special thank you to my grandmother. She had been a barefoot gynecology doctor in a small village in East China for over 50 years. After knowing my thesis topic, she passed on all of her treatment notes to me. She was always keen to know how I was proceeding. Although she did not fully grasp the terms and the theories of my thesis, she offered me special inspiration by telling me many brilliant stories about reproduction treatment from the Republic era to the Post-Mao era.

Prologue

I am not a sweet flower.
I am not a mighty tree.
I am the little grass.
I am the little grass.
Even no one notices me.
Even no one notices me.
——*Little Grass*

This was the third time in one week that I encountered this couple. A man in his 40s was holding a boy and kneeling at the center of the road outside the clinic where I conducted my PhD fieldwork. In front of him was an empty begging bowl. The woman with almost all white hair sat on top of an old van and sang a song called Little Grass into a loudspeaker. Little Grass is a famous Chinese song that borrows grass qualities to express ordinary people's optimism. A group of security guards and police officers surrounded the couple. They did not chase the couple away. Instead, they tried to prevent the couple from talking to onlookers and onlookers from talking to the couple.

Some onlookers told me that the couple came to the clinic almost every day and that sometimes their relatives came too. It was said that the couple had conducted IVF treatment, the mother giving birth to the child in the clinic. Although the clinic did not notice during pregnancy checks, the child was born with cerebra palsy. The couple demanded that the clinic take full responsibility for not identifying the child's illness before his birth, but it declined to do so. The matter was further complicated by the fact that a medical mediation board and a court in Beijing attributed only minor responsibility to the clinic.

An old man walked by and asked a security guard if the couple were swindlers. Hearing this, the couple became angry. The woman (2016) stopped singing immediately and shouted at the old man with her loudspeaker, "I am going to sue you for slander. We used up all our money treating our child," the woman cried. "We have no money anymore. We can only make money by singing. We make money using our own talents. Is it wrong?" In tears, the woman (2016) then complained about their treatment at the hands of the clinic and public officials:

> We did not interfere with the business of the clinic. We just want them to respond to us. I tried appealing to higher authorities such as the Ministry of Health and a court in Beijing. They said they were not

responsible for the case. They sent the police to drive us away. Officials
help one another (*guan guan xiang hu*).

The woman implied that her misery had been caused by irresponsibility and
complicity on the part of the clinic and officials. Hearing this, the old man left
in silence. The woman then continued singing Little Grass until all onlookers
left.

Chapter 1

Introduction

Modern: Relating to the present or recent times as opposed to the remote past.
—*Oxford English Dictionary*

Power technologies

This book is based on the ethnographic research conducted as part of my PhD thesis. Its main purpose is to analyze the policy-making rationale behind regulations of assisted reproductive technologies (ARTs) in China. I also use ARTs as a lens to examine broader changes in Chinese society. In so doing, I show how reproduction and reproductive technologies are enmeshed in social, cultural, moral, and political contexts.

I have opened this book with a medical dispute I witnessed during my PhD fieldwork. I could not verify the authenticity of the couple's story, but I was intrigued by the plausibility of their claims. Thus, I read a few medical articles about the diagnosis of cerebral palsy among newborn babies. According to the study by MacLennan et al. (2015) on the causes and pathways of cerebral palsy, for example, doctors can monitor babies' overall health in order to prevent infections or preexisting conditions that lead to cerebral palsy. Still, diagnosing cerebral palsy during pregnancy is challenging if no preexisting conditions are present. Babies can be diagnosed shortly after birth due to a lack of blood flow or oxygen to their brains during labor (Cerebral Palsy org., 2021). Therefore, it is difficult for clinicians to entirely prevent cerebral palsy before birth.

The couple's claim that the clinic should take full responsibility for their child's illness underscores the high expectations patients seeking fertility treatment often harbor regarding the effectiveness of tests and treatments. Such perceptions are fomented by misleading advertising of ARTs. Indeed, since the birth of Louise Brown in July 1978 in England, ARTs have been associated with miracles in public discourse: a heartbreaking couple who were infertile for many years got the chance to hold babies of their own in their own arms with the help of Intrauterine insemination (IUI); a determined 54 years' old lady finally realized the dream of getting pregnant after a few attempts of in vitro fertilization (IVF) treatment; an open-minded single woman gave birth to a baby through sperm donation. These stories all contribute to the perceptions of ARTs as dream makers.

In her pioneering book studying the personal experience of the first generation of IVF users in the UK, Sarah Franklin defines IVF as a "hope technology" (1997). She argues IVF could bring hope to infertile patients who struggle to find a reproductive solution despite the possibility of treatment failure. According to her, the discourse on hope reflects a broader belief in technology development: the belief that technology can overcome adversity. Building on Franklin's argument on how technology changes people's experience of adversity, I argue that ARTs offer more than hope; they represent power technology that enshrines human agency.

On the one hand, people believe ARTs could allow them to exercise some control over reproduction outcomes. In many ancient societies worldwide, reproduction was attributed to almighty forces beyond human control. For example, ancient Egyptians prayed to Tawaret to protect women in labor (Britannica, 2022). In ancient China, married women offered prayers to the Goddess of Mercy (*guan yin*) in order to get pregnant and give birth to sons (Tian and Huang, 2021). Even as late as 1950, an article published in the Annals of Surgery by doctors Roger Scott and Richard Te Linde suggested that many women had to accept infertility as "God's will or fate's bidding" (1950, p.697). With the development of reproductive science, however, human reproduction is no longer perceived as solely governed by mysterious blessings and divine curses. For example, Pre-implantation Genetic Testing (PGT-M/SR) allows for the assessment of embryos for genetic diseases, enabling individuals to anticipate and potentially mitigate health conditions arising from genetic predispositions. Though misdiagnosis remains possible, compared to the era before genetic screening, when health conditions were only discovered after childbirth, genetic screening provides a degree of control over offspring health conditions. As sociologist Maren Klawiter has argued, genetic screening "transform[s] human individuality and the uncertainty, unpredictability, and openness of human reproduction into a predetermined, controlled, and regulated assembly line that churns out high-quality, genetically perfect models of human beings" (1990, p.82).

On the other hand, reproductive science removes many biological barriers to reproductive autonomy. For example, many women experience a decline in fertility starting at age 30 (ACOG, 2020), with a significant reduction in ovarian reserve by age 40 (Wallace and Kelsey, 2010) and minimal chances of live births by age 45 (Leridon, 2005). Hence, many women face pressure from this pregnancy's biological clock. For those postponing childbearing for whatever reasons, egg freezing provides the possibility of pausing their biological clock. Since a woman's fertility is affected by the age of her eggs rather than her uterus, women freeze unfertilized eggs when they are younger for use when they are older. This procedure mitigates many of the risks of bearing children later in one's life (Baldwin et al., 2014). Though egg freezing still cannot guarantee live births, it, to some extent, allows women to dodge the fear of "anticipated infertility" (Martin, 2010, p.526) when they deviate from seemingly natural, self-evident patterns of marriage and childbearing.

The world's first IVF baby was born in the UK in 1978, and the first successful pregnancy after intracytoplasmic sperm injection (ICSI) occurred in Belgium in 1992. Nowadays, ARTs have traveled from Europe to various parts of the world, where millions of individuals and couples engage in technologically supported endeavors to achieve conception. China, which formerly implemented strict birth control policies, surprisingly ranks among the world's most prolific ART nations.[1] According to an unprecedented analysis from the Ministry of Health, from 2013 to 2016, the total number of ART (IVF, ICSI, FET, PGT) cycles nationwide remarkably increased from 490,680 (National Health and Family Planning Commission, 2015) to 906, 840 (Bai et al., 2020).[2,3] In comparison, in the higher-value U.S. market, a total of 160,521 ART cycles were performed in 467 American fertility clinics (Sunderam et al., 2015), while 263,577 cycles were recorded in 2016 (Center for Disease Control, 2018).

Similar to how ARTs are advertised in Europe and America, in China, ARTs are also promoted for their magic power in media and clinical promotion materials. For instance, an article about the life stories of Professor Guangxiu Lu, a key researcher in China's first IVF project, published by the Human Province government, depicted IVF as a modern manifestation of the Goddess of Mercy (*guan yin*) (Hunan Province Government, 2006).

---

[1] In China, birth control policies refer to the One-Child Policy which was enforced after 1979.

[2] Since 1954, the Ministry of Health has been responsible for the national health portfolio. The Ministry of Health superseded in 2013 by the National Health and Family Planning Commission. In 2018, the National Health and Family Planning Commission was dissolved and that its functions were integrated into the National Health Commission. In this book, I use the Ministry of Health when I describe the government agency before 2013. I use the National Health and Family Planning Commission (NHFPC) when I describe the government agency between 2013 and 2018. And I use the National Health Commission when I describe the government agency after 2018.

[3] It's worth noting that 2016 marked the introduction of the Two-Children Policy, which could have contributed to the increased demand for ARTs, particularly among older women seeking a second child. While there isn't available data beyond 2016, a comparison between ART utilization rates in China and the United States during the period from 2013 to 2016 suggests a consistent trend in China.

The boom in ARTs in China is not solely attributed to their role in granting power over reproduction but also their contribution to national power, as envisioned by Chairman Deng Xiaoping.[4] National power, encompassing various elements such as natural resources, economic development, technological advancement, and cultural influence, is regarded as a measure of a country's comprehensive development and international standing (Zheng, 1998). It has been important in the political thought in China since Mao's era, but its meaning changes with different political leaders' visions. For instance, emphasizing "political power grows out of the barrel of a gun" (Mao, 2019), Chairman Mao Zedong promoted political consolidation and military strength in order for China to survive (*sheng cun wen ti*).[5] On the contrary, in Deng's era, development issues (*fa zhan wen ti*) such as technological innovation and population quality became his main focus.

Technological innovation is a cornerstone of national power, and China's achievements in ARTs exemplify its successful technological development under Deng's leadership. Countries are keen to race to be first to develop new or frontier technologies (Bharadwaj, 2002; Franklin and Roberts, 2006) to show their national power. Louise Brown or Dolly the sheep are perhaps the most well-known "firsts" of the United Kingdom. China is no exception.

Funding ARTs research by the government began in China in the early 1980s. In Hunan Medical School, on 26 January 1983, a baby girl was born using IUI. She was the first baby to be born in China with the help of ARTs. Her birth encapsulated the development of technology. As Chinastory—an official media source—remarks, "The success of IUI marked a new beginning for technology and indicates that China is catching up with Europe and America" (Liu, Hong, and Dong, 2020). Similarly, *People's Daily*, an official Chinese media source, commented on the test-tube baby's birth in 1988: "Her first cry not only marked the birth of a new life but also reflected the breakthrough of modern medical technology in China" (1988).

While IUI and IVF success in China trailed behind developed countries by a few years, egg freezing was studied by Chinese scientists as early as scientists in developed countries. Human egg freezing trials began at Peking University ARTs Clinic in 2003, culminating in the successful birth of a child in 2004 (Chen and Cai, 2007). Researchers impregnated seven women with fertilized frozen

---

[4] After Chairman Zedong Mao died in 1976, Chairman Xiaoping Deng gradually rose to power. During his administration from 1978 to 1992, he launched several modernization programs in China, including economic reforms and the One-Child Policy. His far-reaching reforms earned him the reputation as the "architect of modern China."

[5] Zedong Mao was the founding father of the People's Republic of China. He was the Chairman of the Chinese Communist Party from 1949 until his death in 1976.

eggs. One of these women successfully gave birth to a child in 2004, which marked the first successful use of egg freezing in China (Chen and Cai, 2007).[6] Human eggs contain a lot of water, which can easily crystallize during freezing (Mullen, Rosenbaum, and Critser, 2007). However, Chinese scientists claimed to have solved this difficulty independently of international researchers. As Honglin Xu, a Chinese ARTs expert, wrote, "Peking University Medical School conducted experiment independently for two years using a slow freezing and quick thawing technique. Scientists put frozen eggs into a highly concentrated sugar liquid, and accordingly, the survival rate of thawing eggs became as high as 96%" (2004, p.65). Chinese scientists' independent solutions to technical challenges showcased Indigenous innovation in egg freezing technology, a hallmark of China's technological prowess.

Nowadays, Chinese science closely rivals leading research on reproductive technologies globally. An interviewee recommended a book called Ethics and Management of ARTs ("The *Book*").[7] She informed me that clinicians made ethical decisions according to it. Hence, the *Book* was an important reading material for understanding how ARTs should be conducted in China. According to the *Book*,

> The first IVF baby in the world was born in the United Kingdom in 1978, ten years earlier than the first IVF baby in China. However, the first egg freezing baby in China was born in 2004, only five years later than the world's first live birth using frozen eggs. The first ICSI baby was born at the First Medical School of Zhongshan University in 1996 in Guangzhou, only four years later than the first ICSI baby in Belgium (Yu et al., 2015, p5).

The *Book* demonstrates that China has already reduced its lag behind other developed countries in science and technology by reaching an internationally leading level in fertility treatment. ARTs provide China with a means of achieving power and status in the international community.

---

[6] In July 2003 Dr. Xiaohong Li, who worked at Peking University's ARTs Clinic, had impregnated the baby's mother using donated frozen eggs from the egg bank. The mother was 38 years of age and infertile due to ovarian hypofunction. Her baby was born in Jiangsu Province on 29 April 2004, weighing four kilograms. At that time, egg bank was allowed. However, the egg bank did not last long due to shortage of eggs.

[7] Dr. D recommended this *Book* to me, I was unable to visit P Clinic's ethics committee, for its members felt uncomfortable about being observed. However, Dr. D was a member of the committee. As such, she informed me that they made decisions according to the *Book*, which had been edited by the MOH and Peking University Medical College. It details the ways in which ARTs should be conducted in China.

In addition to technology, population quality was also considered a measure of a country's national power during the Deng era. China introduced the One-Child Policy in 1978 to relieve the burden that a large population placed upon food production and raise people's living standards (Chen, 1981). Under the One-Child Policy, each Chinese couple of Han Ethnicity must have only one child. Later, the government noted that not only population quantity but also population quality (*ren kou su zhi*) is essential to the country's development. The government's rationale was that since each couple could conceive only one child, the child should be healthy and clever.

Efforts to enhance population quality included eugenic campaigns (Handwerker, 2002).[8] For example, the government "encouraged technological developments in the field of reproduction, launched programs on infant and maternal health-care, [provided] medical information on genetic disorders..." (Dikötter, 1998, p.123). In addition, the government encouraged Late Marriage and Late Childbearing (*wan hun wan yu*), providing extra annual leave for women who postponed marriage until the age of 23 and men who did so after 25.[9] It also provided additional maternal leave for women who conceived their children after the age of 24.[10] These incentives encouraged couples to devote

---

[8] In western narratives, there are two types of eugenics. One is negative eugenics, which tries to reduce the number of genetically undesirable people. The other is positive eugenics which tries to increase the number of genetically desirable people. The notion of eugenics was introduced into China in the late nineteenth century, leading to several translations of the term. Scholar Fu Yan translated it as "the theory of having good babies" (*zhe si xue*) in April 1898. In 1902, Scholar Binghan Zhang used the term "the theory of modifying human races" (*ren zhong gai zao xue*). Scholar Songhua Yu's 1919 translation – "the theory of good childbirth" (*you sheng xue*) – became widely accepted.
The concept of eugenics in China is completely different to that which prevailed in the United States during the Progressive Era and that characteristic of Nazi Germany. When Guangdan Pan introduced the basic principles of eugenics into China, he tried to steer clear of notions of racism and colonialism. In a book titled *Modern History of Racism*, Pan argues that social choice theory is not directly related to racism (Pan, 1995). In addition, Chinese eugenics programs paid attention to the importance of nurture and environment rather than simply emphasizing race and genes. Indeed, the government developed modern technology in maternal and prenatal care, developed policies to support the disabled people, and promoted education on reproduction.
[9] According to the Marriage Law, the minimum legal age for marriage is 22 years for men and 20 years for women.
[10] The national legislation did not specify how long this additional maternity leave should. Instead, conditions and time frames were finalized depending on individual situations and regions. For this reason, additional maternity leave ranged between seven days and three months.

more time to their careers and education in order to become psychologically mature and financially prepared to raise children (Wu, 1997).

Funding research on ARTs was among these eugenic strategies. For example, in late 1983, the Family Planning Department of the provincial government in Hunan province organized an exhibition titled "Superior Births" (*you sheng*) (Franklin and Roberts, 2006). Participants at the exhibition discussed sperm banking as a method of improving population quality. Then, in the 1990s, the Family Planning Department in Chengdu, Sichuan Province, funded the first celebrity sperm bank in China. The sperm bank emphasized eugenics, encouraging scholars and film stars to donate sperm in order to produce babies with desirable physical traits. Though the sperm bank was banned later due to concerns over negative eugenics, the government initially perceived artificial insemination as a potential means to improve population quality in China rather than solely as a treatment for infertility.

Similarly, IVF research received governmental funding under the guise of eugenics. Initially, China's first IVF project aimed at helping infertile women whose fallopian tubes were blocked to conceive children.[11] However, conducting IVF research under the One-Child Policy raised contradictions, with some questioning its necessity given China's large population. As Professor Lizhu Zhang put it, "There were other voices at the time. Some people said China already has such a huge population, so why do you still want to work on test-tube babies? They said this went against the national family planning policies" (Wahlberg, 2016, p.102). To handle the skepticism, researchers titled the funding application for the IVF project in Eugenics: The Protection, Preservation, and Development of Early Embryos (*you sheng, zao qi pei tai de bao hu, bao cun he fa zhan*) to satisfy officials' increasing interest in population quality on the part of family planning (Greenhalgh and Winckler, 2005).

---

[11] Professor Lizhu zHANG, of Peking University Third Hospital, found that 50% of Chinese infertile women had blocked fallopian tubes (Scharping, 2013). There are several reasons for these blockages, such as unsafe abortion procedures, abdominal or pelvic surgery, gynecological inflammation, sexually transmitted diseases, and bacterial infections contracted during menstruation. Prior to the 1980s, standards of hygiene and medical care were low in China, resulting in a high rate of fallopian tube blockage. Many patients' fallopian tubes were already too fragile for tubal anastomosis surgery. Drawing on experiences that she had gained while studying abroad, Zhang thought that IVF might help these patients. Along with Professor Huilin Lu and Guangxiu Lu of Central South University Xiangya Hospital, and Professor Cuihua He of Peking Union Medical College Hospital, Zhang prepared and submitted a grant application on IVF to the National Natural Science Foundation of China.

Egg freezing also aligned with the government's demographic goals of improving population quality. According to Sina's report on the first successful case of egg freezing in China (2004), the government supported women interested in trying egg freezing technology by offering discounted fees to promote late marriage and late childbearing as part of the One-Child Policy.[12] The government claimed that egg freezing suits women who wish to delay childbirth but eventually conceive healthy babies.

Controversial regulations

Although ARTs are celebrated as power technologies that aligned with policy agendas in the Deng era, the government has set up a few barriers to accessing the technologies. In 1999, the Department of Science and Education in the Ministry Of Health (MOH) assessed the safety, effectiveness, ethics, and economic costs of ARTs. It introduced four classifications of medical technology, distinguishing among technologies that should be encouraged, limited, explored, and prohibited. ARTs belong to the technology that should be limited. In 2001 and 2003, the MOH further set up the conditions to use ARTs by issuing the Management Policies on ARTs (*ren lei fu zhu sheng zhi ji shu guan li ban fa*), the Management Policies on Sperm Banks (*ren lei jing zi ku guan li ban fa*), the Regulations on ARTs (*ren lei fu zhu sheng zhi ji shu gui fan*), the Basic Standards for Sperm Banks (*ren lei jing zi ku ji ben biao zhun*), the Technology Standards for Sperm Banks (*ren lei jing zi ku ji shu gui fan*), the Ethical Review Principles in Performing ARTs (*shi shi ren lei fu zhu sheng zhi ji shu de lun li yuan ze*), the Ethical Principles for Sperm Banks (*ren lei jing zi ku lun li yuan ze*), and the Review and Approval Process for ARTs and Sperm Banks (*ren lei fu zhu sheng zhi ji shu he ren lei jing zi ku lun li yuan ze*).

Among various conditions, three access criteria are highly controversial. This book aims to uncover the rationale behind these criteria. The first, what I term the medicalization criteria, stipulates that ARTs should primarily be applied in medical situations. The second, the marriage criteria, grants access to most ARTs exclusively to married individuals. Lastly, the doctor-patient relationship criteria outline patient management during fertility treatment. In the following sections, I elaborate on how these three criteria spark debates and scrutiny.

The medicalization criteria

Central to ART access decisions is the question of whether people have a medical need. Many countries adopt a binary "medical V.S. social" approach when determining eligibility for fertility treatment. For example, according to

---

[12] Sina is a Chinese media company. It operates Sina Weibo and Sina News.

medical guidelines in the United Kingdom (UK), infertility is regarded as a medical condition to be addressed through ARTs (NICE, 2020). Consequently, individuals without medically diagnosed infertility cannot access fertility treatment through the National Health Service (NHS), although they may seek private treatment.

Similarly, Chinese regulations emphasize that clinicians must adhere strictly to medical indications when determining whether to perform ARTs on patients. In other words, clinicians should only treat patients who show medical conditions such as infertility or genetic problems. For instance, according to the Regulations on ARTs, the indications for IVF should be limited to oocyte transport disorder, ovulation disorder, Endometriosis, asthenospermia, unexplained infertility, and immune infertility. Egg freezing is also permitted solely for medical reasons in China. While the national regulations do not specify the medical indications for egg freezing, local regulatory documents outline the specific conditions. For instance, according to the Notice on Conducting Quality Control on Human Assisted Reproductive Technology Service Projects in the City (*guan yu zuo hao ben shi ren lei fu zhu sheng zhi ji shu fu wu xiang mu zhi liang kong zhi de tong zhi*) implemented by Shanghai Municipal Health and Family Planning Commission in 2013, egg freezing is permitted in only two situations—the first it can be conducted in cases of couples having to undergo infertility treatment. If the husband's sperm is disqualified on the day of gamete retrieval, clinicians will freeze the wife's eggs instead. Second, patients suffering from cancers or tumors who wish to preserve their fertility can freeze eggs prior to surgery and chemoradiotherapy (Zhang and Ren, 2016). Both situations imply that the social use of egg freezing among healthy women is not allowed.

Medicalization is a process by which a social or human problem is defined as a medical one. Extensive academic study has examined the challenges associated with medicalizing ARTs. On the one hand, medicalization can create social pressure. For instance, restricting access to ARTs for healthy homosexual couples reflects social discrimination against homosexual parenthood (Bell, 2014). For infertile patients, medicalization can induce anxiety as they perceive involuntary childlessness as a disease requiring a cure (Ergin et al., 2018).

On the other hand, the boundary between medical use and social use of ARTs is often ambiguous. Consider women's age-related infertility as an example. Advanced maternal age is associated with decreased fertility, obstetric and gynecological complications, and increased risk of miscarriage (Baird et al., 2005). Women may delay childbearing due to lifestyle factors such as pursuing a professional career or not finding the right partner (Hodes-Wertz, 2013; Stanton and Sussman, 2014; Waldby, 2015; Inhorn, 2017; Baldwin et al., 2019). Egg freezing is proposed as a form of preventive medicine for these women, allowing them to preserve healthy eggs when they are young for later use. Borovecki et al. (2018) argue against hierarchies between medical reasons and social motivations, suggesting that if fertility preservation among oncological patients is viewed positively, egg freezing to protect professional women against ovarian aging should not be restricted.

This book investigates why Chinese regulations prioritize medical purposes for ARTs and how clinicians address age-related fertility decline in clinical practice. It examines whether the side effects of ARTs justify these criteria. Additionally, it explores the gendered nature of the medicalization criteria, analyzing discrepancies between the requirement for women in Shanghai to have sufficient medical reasons to freeze eggs and the permission of men to freeze sperm for personal reasons under the Basic Standards for Sperm Banks.

The marriage criteria

The regulations in China restrict single women's access to ARTs. The key intervention at the national level comes in the fourth clause of a regulation titled Ethical Review Principles for Performing ARTs, which asserts that clinics cannot perform ARTs on single women. Another is found in the thirteenth clause of another directive, Regulations on ARTs, according to which clinics cannot perform ARTs on couples or single women who cannot conceive children according to family planning policies.[13]

In practice, the second clause of the Regulations on ARTs mandates clinics to carefully verify patients' marriage certificates and birth permission certificates before they conduct treatment. Foreigners must also adhere to these regulations by providing marriage certificates. In addition, Basic Standards for Sperm Banks indicate that women must present marriage certificates when applying for sperm. "Sperm banks should not be used for unmarried women's assisted reproductive treatment," the *Book* states. "Unmarried women include single women, widowed women, divorced women, and homosexual women" (Yu et al., 2015, p.100).[14]

---

[13] Family planning policies refer to the One-Child Policy.
[14] The Rainbow Society, an non-government organization advocating single women's reproduction rights, published a report on single women's access to fertility services in China in 2016. It tried to consult twenty sperm banks in China in producing their annual report. Three banks were unapproachable; the other 17 only allowed married couples to apply for sperm (Rainbow Society, 2016, p.14). The Report found that many voluntary single mothers inject sperm either procured from acquaintances or purchased on the black market. The quality of the sperm sold on the black market is not guaranteed, however. And although some single women seek donated sperm from foreign reproduction agencies, this is expensive.

Jilin Province stands out as the only area of China to decree that "childless women who reach the legal age of marriage and decide not to get married can use ARTs to have one child" (The Standing Committee of People's Congress, 2002).[15] However, although a woman can sign an agreement promising that she will not marry in the future, these agreements are difficult to enforce because the condition of marriage itself is puzzling. Consequently, since the enactment of the Jilin Legislation, only one single woman successfully conceived children with ARTs in Jilin Province.[16]

Many people argue that the marriage criteria deprive single women of reproductive rights. Indeed, in August 2015, Xu Jinglei, a famous Chinese actress, criticized the ARTs regulations on Sina Weibo (a Chinese version of Twitter). She froze eggs in the U.S. because the Chinese government did not allow single women to use ARTs. Her egg freezing experience garnered widespread public attention and immediately prompted intense online protests against the marriage criteria. Subsequently, there was a scholarly debate on single women's reproduction rights. For instance, legal scholar Xin He (2015) demonstrated that women own their eggs and have the right to freeze them regardless of their marital status. Similarly, medical scholar Lei Li (2016) characterized eggs as a special form of private property, affirming women's autonomy in deciding how to use their eggs.

This book analyzes why the regulations in China restrict single women from accessing ARTs and examines officials' and clinicians' understanding of the implications of marriage in reproduction and fertility treatment. Moreover, it explores the gendered nature of the marriage criteria, highlighting that while national regulations emphasize women's marital status in pursuing IVF, freezing eggs, or using donated sperm, they do not impose marriage as a prerequisite for sperm freezing. The Basic Standards for Sperm Banks identify two situations in which men are eligible for sperm freezing. In the first, men undergo infertility treatment. In the second, men can freeze sperm for fertility preservation before receiving teratogenic doses of radiation, drugs, toxic

---

[15] In China, local legislation is subsidiary to the Constitution and the national laws, but they have the same force as the policies and regulations issued by government agencies. The Jilin Legislation was passed by the local People's Congress, while the national regulations on ARTs were issued by the Ministry of Health. Therefore, the Jilin Legislation has the same force as the national regulations on ARTs.

[16] Also, in Jilin Province – the only province that allows single women to use ARTs – clinics still hesitate in offering the service to single women. According to the report from Rainbow Society, since 2002, only one single woman in Jilin Province hospitals has successfully accessed ARTs.

substances, sterilizations, or personal reasons. Neither situation requires men to be married.

The doctor-patient relationship criteria

Fertility treatment is recognized as a significant source of stress for patients and may result in the cessation of treatment (Gameiro et al., 2012). Studies have demonstrated that a good doctor-patient relationship plays a pivotal role in patients' decision-making, treatment compliance, and retention in fertility treatment, while a poor relationship leads to treatment discontinuation or clinic switching (Malin et al., 2001; Leite et al., 2005; Dancet et al., 2011; Gameiro et al., 2012). Poor doctor-patient relationship is frequently reported in the literature on fertility treatment. For example, patients often complain about inadequate explanations of fertility issues, insufficient attention to psychological well-being (Gameiro et al., 2012), incomplete provision of information (Haagen et al., 2008), inadequate support for managing stress (Olivius et al., 2004), negative interactions with staff (Rajkhowa et al., 2006), and insufficient focus on patient-centric care (van Empel et al., 2011).

To foster positive doctor-patient relations, countries implement laws and policies regarding patient management. The doctor-patient criteria outlined in ARTs regulations in China aim to mitigate medical disputes during fertility treatment. According to Ethical Principles for Sperm Banks and Review and Approval Process for ARTs and Sperm Banks, for example, clinicians are mandated to provide patients with comprehensive information on available options, treatment advantages and disadvantages, and associated risks. They must also disclose treatment costs and potential outcomes. Treatment should not be proposed unless patients are fully informed. Furthermore, clinics are required to regularly organize public education programs to disseminate knowledge about conception and infertility in an easily understandable manner. Clinicians are instructed to refrain from using hurtful, negatively suggestive, or ambiguous language during consultations.

At first glance, this requirement for patient management benefits patients. However, it is not well-received among clinicians. Clinicians argue that this requirement strains already overcrowded state-run hospitals. Fertility clinics in China are rammed with people. As I mentioned earlier, there were nearly a million treatment cycles conducted in approved clinics in China in 2016 alone. Due to the overwhelming demand, clinicians have less time to dedicate to patient management compared to actual treatment. A fertility specialist in a public clinic told me during our interview, "We are too busy now. We do not have enough hospital beds. The government only subsidizes each extra bed to the tune of ¥500. Many fundamental problems are unsolved. How can we have time to consider these requests......" She implied that following the doctor-patient relationship criteria proposed by these regulations is unrealistic due to a shortage of medical resources.

Considering clinician's responses to the doctor-patient relationship criteria during our interviews, I examine why the doctor-patient relationship criteria remain applicable despite being deemed infeasible by clinicians. I am also curious about the implementation of these criteria in extremely busy clinical settings. This entails examining how clinicians disclose bad news, inform patients of knowledge gaps, and manage medical disputes when issues arise.

Spiral modernization

While ARTs represent not only human control over reproduction but also the expansion of China's national power during the Deng era, current regulations suggest they can easily provoke medical disputes and should primarily be confined to medical settings, particularly for married women. Reflecting on the development and marketing of ARTs in China, I find the criteria for medicalization, marriage, and doctor-patient relationship indeed puzzling. First, though ARTs symbolize the omnipotence of human power, Chinese regulations largely restrict their use to medical contexts. Second, though the government promotes ARTs to improve overall population quality, most ARTs are only open to married people. Third, although Chinese clinicians have demonstrated great expertise in developing ARTs, there are still concerns about their management of these technologies in clinical settings. The book uncovers the reasoning and tactics behind the criteria for providing fertility treatment and related practices in Chinese clinics.

Existing scholarly work (Huang, 2006; Lu, 2008; He, 2015; Wang et al., 2015; Zhang, 2016; Yang and Pan, 2016; Lian, 2016; Zhang and Ren, 2016; Li, 2016) on Chinese ARTs regulations tends to focus on the question of whether technologies should be allowed or not. For example, Wang, Huang, and Liu (2015) were concerned that the wide application of egg freezing would delay women's marriage and childbearing age and thereby compound the issue of China's aging population. Zhang and Ren (2016) argue that allowing single women to freeze eggs would be incompatible with the One-Child Policy. These studies merely present value judgments and put forward viewpoints on how ARTs *should* be conducted rather than attending to how it *is* conducted. These perspectives are decontextualized, indeed transcendental. This book makes a distinctive and substantial contribution to the existing literature by moving beyond a strictly legalistic account of ARTs in China. It takes a step back to examine the logic underlying regulations on ARTs and their implementation in clinics.

The primary theme that emerged from my ethnography was the prevalence of uncertainty in the discourse and practices of ARTs in China. Firstly, the use of ARTs was primarily restricted to medical settings due to the inherent uncertainty associated with these technologies and the unanswered questions surrounding their outcomes. For example, some clinicians I interviewed felt uncertain about the outcomes of ARTs for individual cases. They could not guarantee that successful embryo transplantation would definitely lead to successful childbirth. Secondly, women's marital status played a crucial role in avoiding single motherhood, as it could lead to uncertainty regarding children's paternity, according to some policymakers. Thirdly, disputes between infertility patients and clinicians, as well as between single mothers and officials, were common. Some patients, for example, expressed uncertainty about treatment outcomes due to inadequate clinical services.

However, my interviewees went beyond discussing the concept of uncertainty itself. When I asked about their views on ARTs regulations, they often related the uncertainty of ARTs to broader national issues such as fertility decline, shortcomings of the medical system, and social unrest, many of which were seen as side effects of Chairman Deng's modernization policies. Such views cropped up frequently during my fieldwork. Therefore, when I interpreted my interviewees' narratives of uncertainty, the first challenging question was whether their comments on Chairman Deng's modernization policies were distracting. I do not view their arguments as missing the specific subject of my questions, ARTs. ARTs correspond to China's modernization plans in the Deng era- not merely in that they were developed during Chairman Deng's leadership. The discourse on ARTs aligns with many of Chairman Deng's modernization strategies, such as technology development and the One-Child Policy. My interviewees' arguments suggest that ARTs provide a lens through which to appraise broader social changes in China.

Then, the second challenging question I encountered was how to precisely describe and theorize the relationship between the uncertainty of ARTs and the broader picture of China's national development. Having situated the development of ARTs amid China's modernization trajectory, my interviewees implied that the uncertainty surrounding ARTs reflects drawbacks of the modernization strategies implemented during the Deng era, such as technological misuse, late marriage, late childbearing, and imbalanced distribution of medical resources. Ultimately, I decided to characterize this book as an overarching sociological analysis of how responses to ARTs help delineate key features of contemporary Chinese society.

The uncertainty of ARTs that my interviewees articulated offers a window into the intricacies of China's modernization path. In English, modernity means both a historical period from the twelfth and thirteenth centuries in Europe and certain sociocultural values stemming from the Renaissance and the Enlightenment. Since the Renaissance, significant scientific advancements have occurred in European societies, culminating in the Industrial Revolution, which revolutionized modes of production. Political revolutions underscored principles of constitutionalism and democracy. When the concept of modernity was introduced into China by reformers who, from the end of the Opium Wars in the 1860s onwards, sought to rescue China's strategic position, they widened the horizon of thinking about modernity. For them, to become modern was to break away from China's colonial past and catch up with advanced Western nations. Therefore, though they endorsed modern values such as science and democracy, they preferred the term "modernization" (*xian dai hua*) over "modernity" (*xian dai xing*). This is because they adopted modern values in order to propel China's development. This distinction underscores the developmental aspect of modernization. Chinese modernization was passive and traumatic. Moreover, the main purpose of Chinese modernization is the growth of national power. As Chinese Marxist scholar Xinxia Chen has written, "modernization in China was forced by Western armies. The society modernized in order to fight against the foreign invasion and survive" (2017, p. 30). Without keeping this history of colonial encroachment in mind, it would be impossible to understand the Chinese interpretation of modernization.

From the late Qing Dynasty to the rule of the Chinese Communist Party (CCP), successive governments formulated diverse modernization strategies in order to transform China from a traditional, impoverished society to a modern, prosperous country. Among these, Chairman Deng's reformist government in the late 1970s spearheaded the Four Modernizations (*si ge xian dai hua*) initiative, which helped China become a major world economic power. Scientific and technological development was critical to Chairman Deng's breakthrough plans. These have involved importing technologies, sending Chinese scientists abroad, building high-tech parks across the country, promoting innovation among state-owned firms, and guaranteeing intellectual property (Zhang, 1992). Besides technological development, attempts to improve population quality formed another crucial part of Chairman Deng's strategies. He believed individuals' healthy birth practices would improve overall population quality, thus bolstering China's status and eradicating its image as the "sick man of Asia" (*dong ya bing fu*), a legacy of historical humiliation. The government, therefore, developed policies to support disabled people, encouraged pre-marriage health checks, and funded modern technology in maternal and prenatal care.

Chinese reformers developed modernization policies in response to evolving societal challenges, resulting in a heterogeneous landscape of modernization efforts marked by struggles and inconsistencies. The shifting government stance towards Western culture serves as a case in point. The New Cultural Movement during the Republican Era (1912-1949) embraced Western values, promoting science and democracy while distancing itself from traditional Chinese culture. However, with Chairman Mao's ascension to power, traditional culture was denounced, and Western culture was branded bourgeois. Deng's subsequent Open and Reform Policy (*gai ge kai fang*) reversed Mao's approach, embracing Western investment and culture. This vacillation between acceptance and rejection of Western influences typifies the complex dynamics of modernization policies.

In this study, my interviewees' reflections on Deng's modernization policies vis-à-vis ARTs underscore this key aspect of China's modernization trajectory: the coexistence of policy reversals and continuities. For example, while clinicians continued treating infertility with ARTs, they highlighted technology uncertainty in order to mitigate over-reliance. In addition, though the government still views ARTs as effective methods of improving population quality, my interviewees introduced the concept of paternal uncertainty to discourage new family forms such as single motherhood. Also, while the government continues developing ARTs strategically in order to bolster China's global standing, it remains wary of medical disputes stemming from patient uncertainty regarding treatment plans.

The co-existence between continuity and reversals in a modern society poses a profound challenge to sociological theories. One paradigm views social development as linear, cohesive, and evolutionary, with modernity being the ultimate form of development. As economic theorist Francis Fukuyama argues in the *End of History and the Last Man*, the end of world history means all nations achieve the Western notions of modernity. Western notions of modernity refer to capitalism, rationality, democracy, unfettered individualism, equality, professionalism, and efficiency. These values became the Bible for many developing countries (Scott, 2000). However, this paradigm, often applied to European and American contexts, struggles to explain the reversals observed in Chinese society. In fact, in Chinese, the word "modern" just translates as meaning "the current time" (*xian dai*), a term that lacks the cultural connotations of the English term modernity (Li, 2011). In China, therefore, modernity is not seen as the ultimate value.

Another paradigm of theorizing social development called historical-dynastic cycles (*chao dai xun huan*) is commonly applied to ancient Chinese society. This paradigm portrays traditional Chinese society as a sequence of small circles. When a new dynasty replaced an old dynasty, it referred to characteristics of the previous dynasty without altering essential social structures. This paradigm indicates that the dynasty change from the Qin Dynasty to the Qing Dynasty is repetitive and circular. Each dynasty in Chinese history rises to a political, economic, and cultural peak. It then declines and is replaced by another dynasty (Reischauer, 1965). People of the old dynasty accept the new dynasty easily since they understand that rise and fall are complementary. "No dynasty would last forever but fall amid domestic crisis" (Zarrow, 2006, p.10), and a new dynasty does not fundamentally change the old dynasty. A widely known Chinese proverb, expressed in the sixteenth-century historical novel Romance of the Three Kingdoms, holds that "after a long split, a union will occur; after a long union, a split will occur" (*fen jiu bi he, he jiu bi fen*). Indeed, the Three Kingdoms (*san guo*) (220-280AD) itself is a distinct example of the complimentary relationship between state rise and fall. After 400 years of unity, the central political power of the Han Dynasty collapsed. Han Dynasty was disintegrated into the Three Kingdoms since the Yellow Turban Rebellion. China was reunited under the Sui Dynasty in the sixth century. The Sui Dynasty maintained a similar centralized political system to the Han Dynasty, though it made a few changes, including establishing new ways to recruit officials and redistributing land. While this paradigm elucidates aspects of traditional Chinese society, it falls short in explaining modernization in China, where despite adverse outcomes like technological misuse and declining fertility rates, the government persists in modernization efforts.

My third challenging question was identifying alternative development paradigms open to China that diverge from simply imitating the trajectory of Western modernity or retaining the dynasty cycles of ancient China. Drawing from Hegel's dialectics, I explain the co-existence between policy continuities and reversals through the concept of "spiral modernization." In Hegelian philosophy, dialectics is a movement that leads from an initial position through an opposing position to a new, third position that includes both the initial position and its opposite. This process unfolds in a spiral motion. It shows a status in which contradictions coexist and develop to a higher level. A spiral connotes a rolling, non-sequential form of development in which contemporary society remains, in some sense, continuous with the past even as it looks to the future.

Chinese society develops in neither a linear nor circular fashion. I describe the three steps of the spiral modernization of Chinese society with the terms *modernization, reversals,* and *new forms of modernization*. The spiral begins with the modernization of the original social structure, followed by reversals where policymakers address the drawback of modernization by partially reverting certain aspects of the process. These reversals pave the way for a new social formation, albeit one that retains elements of the original structure. The concept of spiral modernization I propose underscores a growing awareness of the limitations inherent in modernization policies, shaped in part by the uncertainties surrounding ARTs. It encapsulates China's deliberate reversal of some modernization policies at certain junctures.

Ethnography

This book is based on a six-month ethnographic study conducted in Beijing, the capital of China. I selected Beijing as the research site due to its convenient access to leading public ARTs clinics and policy-making institutions. Some readers might question whether findings from a single city can adequately represent China as a whole. To address this concern, I draw upon the insights of sociologist Xueguang Zhou (2010), who studied the local implementation of national family planning policies. Zhou found that local institutions often form strategic alliances in implementing key state policies despite their own interpretations of these policies. Therefore, while I acknowledge the unique characteristics of other regions, this book rests on the premise that the paradoxes and hybrids of ARTs governance in Beijing also prevail in clinics of other parts of China, though to varying degrees and in different forms.

I sought to use as many resources as possible during my fieldwork.[17] This, I hoped, would allow me to grasp a comprehensive picture of how ARTs are practiced and regulated in China. Such an in-depth exploration can best be achieved by means of a multi-site qualitative investigation involving participant observation, interviews, and the analysis of textual materials. Using multiple empirical materials in a single study promises to establish a deep, multifaceted understanding of the phenomenon under review.

The main focus of my ethnography was fertility clinics and regulatory bodies. Given that this book focuses on the reasons that policymakers and clinicians adduced in governance, it seemed that the most appropriate sites for my fieldwork were the bodies that regulate ARTs. My initial plan was to visit public ART clinics, the National Family Planing and Health Commission (NFPHC),

---

[17] Multi-sited ethnography emerged with the development of interdisciplinary studies such as media studies, science and technology studies and cultural studies (Marcus, 1995). And there is tendency toward multi-sited ethnography in the studies of reproductive technologies (Ginsburg, 1996). The choice of sites is subject to a few tracking strategies. For example, Rouse (1991) follows Mexican immigrants across borders to determine various research sites. Ginsburg (1989) follows the stakeholders of the abortion controversy to generate a multi-sited research terrain. Gaines (1991) tracks the conflict between law and media over the legal status of copyrighted cultural products and identifies research sites such as trademark bodies, legislative bodies and culture products producers. I also adopted multi-sited ethnography for this research. And I followed stakeholders of the ARTs regulations such as clinicians, policymakers, and patients to determine the research sites.

and the National People's Congress (NPC). These institutions are closed to academic researchers in China. To gain access, therefore, I needed to foster private relationships with officials and clinicians. The clinicians I got to know had the authority to grant me access to clinics. The policymakers with whom I established relationships, however, could only offer to give confidential interviews and could not allow me to observe their decision-making processes. Beyond clinics and governmental institutions, I also identified other research sites so as to present a full range of situational and interactional contexts (Charmaz, 2000) that relate to the governance of ARTs. These sites included feminist organizations and ARTs agencies, among others. I was able to visit these sites because my friends knew members of staff there.

This book uses ARTs as a window to understand how clinicians and policymakers in China perceive the relationship between technology and society, national development goals, and gender norms. Accordingly, ARTs provide a productive lens through which to unpack the changes in modernization policies in China. I was aware that involving multiple fieldwork sites might present conflicting narratives. Some policymakers might hold conservative attitudes toward ARTs, while activists of single women's reproduction rights might urge more liberalization of the current ARTs regulations. This book does not seek to reconcile these potentially clashing narratives. Instead, it tries to understand how various accounts (e.g., Celebrating ARTs as technology success limiting ARTs' application) together inform social, political, moral, and cultural changes in China.

P Clinic

To understand how the ARTs regulations are implemented in daily clinical practice, I observed ARTs consultation at a public clinic called P Clinic. P Clinic was located in central Beijing. I chose this clinic as my primary fieldwork site because it is a leading fertility treatment center in China. Patients from other parts of China travel to the clinic for consultations on fertility treatment because it offers better services than those available in their hometowns. Moreover, as the clinic is state-owned, its practice of ARTs strictly follows the national regulations, meaning that its clinicians' opinions on both fertility treatment and national regulations promise to be insightful into how clinics operate and implement regulations.

I went to P Clinic on weekday mornings. Although P Clinic opened at 9 a.m., a long queue had already formed outside the building by 9 a.m. each morning. Many patients told me that they had to queue to register with clinicians at 6 a.m. Registration was on a "first come, first serve" basis. If patients failed to get themselves registered in the morning, there would be no later opportunities for them to see a doctor.

Although P Clinic is situated in a modern community, its surroundings convey a mixture of modern and traditional ways of living. Traffic jams on the road in front of P Clinic symbolized the city's accelerating process of urbanization. In addition, businesses along the road (which have thrived due to the great number of patients drawn to the clinic) represented China's opening-up to the forces of economic globalization. Most shops were international franchises, such as KFC and Carrefour. At the same time, traditional Chinese beliefs were on show. Vendors selling Buddha beads and statues were popular among patients. There were also fortunetellers who stopped passersby to offer their palm-reading services.

I met the gatekeeper of the fieldwork site, Dr. D, at a dinner party hosted by a friend. Dr. D is a fertility specialist working at P Clinic and a member of the board of the Chinese Society of Reproductive Medicine (CSRM). Established in 2005, the CSRM issues guidelines for the practice of ARTs in China and helps the MOH and local health authorities manage ARTs. She agreed to participate in the research in the hope that this would help a wider public understand the existing regulations.

After obtaining oral permission from Dr. D, I was able to enter her consulting room and observe how she treated patients.[18] The ways in which clinicians treated patients grappling with infertility more broadly would also inevitably reflect how they perceived marriage, late childbearing, aging, and other relevant issues, all of which promised to shed light on my topic. My role in the consulting room was that of a participant observer. On one hand, as a participant, my goal was to experience clinical settings in the same way as clinicians and patients. How long did consultations take? Were consultation rooms welcoming? Did clinicians answer patients' questions? On the other hand, I kept my distance from clinicians and patients. I noted how clinicians treated patients, how patients reacted to clinicians' attitudes, and how clinicians communicated national regulations to patients. Dr. D also allowed me to accompany her to treatment rooms. Hence, I was able to observe egg retrieval and embryo implantation.

In addition to observing Dr. D's consultation, I interviewed Dr. D. During our hour-long interview, Dr. D touched upon a broad range of topics, from ARTs,

---

[18] Informed consent ensures research participants' rights are not violated. Researchers are required to explain the aim, the methodology and potential harms to research participants in detail before they start research. Signed consent forms indicate participants' willingness to get involved in research. However, I found consent forms caused suspicion and anxiety of participating in my research because my interviewees regarded consent forms as legal documents. Therefore, this research used oral consent rather than signed paper forms.

through technological development in China to China's modernization policies. I have found her perspectives deeply thought-provoking, whether with regard to success rates of fertility treatment, nature, women's destiny, and reproduction policies.

My interactions with other physicians, nurses, secretaries, and other clinic staff were facilitated by Dr. D, who introduced me to them. I had many informal conversations with these people. Additionally, I arranged formal interviews with Drs. L, G, and Z. They are all fertility specialists at P Clinic. While heavily relying on doctors' perspectives from P Clinic might limit the generalizability of their opinions, it contributed to a more nuanced and coherent understanding of ARTs regulations. The ways in which they interpreted ARTs' success rate and risks, understood national population policies and perceived single women's use of ARTs all complemented the observations I made in Dr. D's consultation room.

I interviewed 21 patients seeking fertility treatment in P Clinic. It was difficult to approach patients in the morning since most were busy trying to register. In the afternoons the clinic was less busy, and patients had more time and patience, meaning that I was able to interview them in the waiting lounge. Indeed, this was where most of my conversations with patients took place. Admittedly, these conversations were sometimes disrupted when clinicians called my informants in for consultations or when other patients joined in our conversations.

I was aware that the presence of a researcher might make people seeking fertility treatment feel more anxious and insecure than they otherwise might have. I learned that infertile people—and especially infertile women—suffer emotional distress, low self-esteem, and lower levels of life satisfaction (McCarthy and Chiu, 2011). To offset any stress induced by being taken as the focus of the sociological study, I asked my interviewees to read information sheets and orally consent that they wanted to take part in the research and were happy to provide information. In the meantime, I also offered to answer any questions they had about my research. I made clear that if they were unwilling to take part in my research, answer certain questions, or discuss unpleasant experiences, then they could avoid a particular question or end the interview altogether. In addition, I stressed that I would conceal their real names in both my field notes and later analyses of the data. To my surprise, approaching patients in the waiting lounge was not as difficult as I had expected. Despite the lack of privacy, the waiting lounge became a place in which patients could share their experiences without being judged by either clinicians or society at large.

Although I applied careful ethical scrutiny to interviews by providing interviewees with consent forms and concealing their real names, I was still cautious about my positionality in relation to participants and my analyses (Charmaz, 2008). As an unmarried woman without children, I was both an insider and an outsider with respect to my informants' world. As an insider, I had knowledge of both ARTs and regulations. As an outsider, I did not share similar characteristics in terms of my interviewees' social and economic backgrounds. Whereas some interviewees (such as clinicians) were much more socially, economically, and politically powerful than me, others (such as patients from remote areas) were less powerful. The hierarchy between powerful interviewees and myself was not of much concern to me. The hierarchy at stake in my interactions with socially and economically disadvantaged patients, though, was more significant. They treated me as an authority or a government official.[19] When I asked them about their attitudes toward policies, therefore, some hesitated to answer me.

To reduce the potential impact that these inequalities might have on my interviews, I disclosed details of my own life and experiences. On occasion, I even told my interlocutors of my own marital and maternal status. This not only diminished barriers between myself—a researcher—and participants. It also helped to draw participants into engaging with topics such as motherhood, reproductive decisions, and natural parenting. On hearing that I was single, one interviewee urged me to conceive children early in life. She then told the story of her twenty-nine-year-old niece, who married in later life and shared her attitudes toward late marriage. I sometimes expressed my own ambivalence toward a particular topic, which led to further disclosures on the part of the interviewees. Nevertheless, in my analyses, I have endeavored to present my interviewees' accounts accurately, not least by providing verbatim quotations. I tried not to influence my interviewees' attitudes by not sharing my perceptions of ARTs or ARTs regulations with them.

Regulatory bodies

As I have mentioned above, my initial plan was to visit the NFPHC and the NPC, the legislative and regulatory bodies responsible for formulating national regulations on ARTs. I was unable to conduct fieldwork in these policy-making agencies, however, for they do not admit external academic researchers. Nevertheless, I still spent a day looking at them from the outside to get a sense of their surroundings. The surroundings indicate the gap between ordinary people and government officials. The NFPHC, for example, is located in central Beijing. The red flag fluttering at the front of the building suggests that it houses a governmental agency. An electric gate is installed outside, and a few security

---

[19] In China, many people equal research interviews with formal interviews from state media. Hence they regard interviewers as government officials.

guards register visitors. Only visitors who have written consent from officials of the NFPHC can enter the building. The Reception Office of the NPC, which receives letters, calls, and visits from individuals or groups who are concerned about making suggestions, filing complaints, or airing grievances, also maintains distance from the public. Hidden in a few residential blocks, the office is very low-key, with only a small white billboard outside bearing its name. What is more, like the NFPHC, the office is set apart by an electric gate, meaning that the public cannot enter into the building at will. Security guards and a police car stand by to ward off the danger that petitioners might initiate a potentially destabilizing protest. Indeed, during my visit I saw a few petitioners gathering outside the building, holding up posters and carrying legal letters documenting their cases. Some policemen tried to persuade them to leave.

Thanks to my friend's introduction, I was able to interview 3 officials: Official H from the NFPHC, Official Q from a local family planning department, and Legislator Y from the NPC.[20] The process of identifying policymakers to interview was circuitous; after I had interviewed Official H, for example, I realized that officials in the family planning department issued the birth permission certificates necessary for ARTs treatment and decided whether single mothers could register children in their household. Therefore, I tried to approach Official Q in the family planning department.

One might ask why I did not include the policymakers who designed the ARTs regulations in 2003. I had to acknowledge that it was very difficult to identify officials who formulated the regulations. Given that the regulations were still in effect, I approached Official H, who approves and manages medical technologies and Legislator Y, who reviews various policies and regulations, including the family planning policies. They provided insights into how the ARTs regulations fit into the current policy-making framework. More importantly, I aim to provide a detailed analysis of the social, cultural, and political implications of the ARTs regulations rather than merely legal and ethical accounts. These officials' voices shed light on how they envision social changes in contemporary Chinese society.

Other fertility actors

In addition to public clinics and regulatory bodies, which are the main actors in regulating ARTs in China, there are other fertility actors in these broader

---

[20] The family planning department refers to National Population and Family Planning Commission and its local branches. Its function was merged into the National Health and Family Planning Commission of the People's Republic of China in 2013. And it was dissolved in 2018.

social, institutional, and cultural contexts. My main reason for continuing my fieldwork beyond the clinic and regulatory bodies was to grasp the full set of contexts that bear upon the ways in which ARTs are regulated in China.

In setting out to explore these actors, my first destination was a private hospital called J Hospital. Around P Clinic, I encountered men distributing leaflets for illegal fertility services and medicines. Prompted by these advertisements, I was curious to find out whether private clinics can really disobey the regulations on ARTs and conduct treatment that public clinics cannot. Then, I met a woman who was the landlord of a patient seeking fertility treatment at P Clinic. She introduced J Hospital. Surprisingly, despite providing illegal services such as egg trading and sex selection, J Hospital said they had a medical license. Upon learning of this, I became interested in how ARTs were practiced in a private hospital that operated in a legal gray area.

Thanks to the referral from the woman, I visited J Hospital, accompanied by Dr. W, a specialist working there. It was difficult to find J Hospital, which was "hidden" in a residential site. No one queued in front of it, and the waiting lounge was almost empty. Dr. W told me that their patients did not need to make appointments in advance; patients could meet clinicians after paying a registration fee of ¥100. I spent one day at the hospital, during which it became clear what was allowed and what was not. I interviewed Dr. W to ascertain her understanding of ART policies.

I also identified the important role played by ARTs agencies. The unavailability of many fertility services due to strict regulations makes patients turn to overseas clinics. Japan, countries in South Asia, and the United States are the most popular destinations for "repro-travel" (Inhorn, 2013). It is difficult for Chinese patients and overseas clinics to work together due to language barriers and information asymmetries. Agencies, then, provide a bridge between them. By visiting these agencies, I hoped to understand how their employees viewed the restrictions of certain fertility treatments, such as single women's access to ARTs. One informant had worked with a clinic in California (C Agency); the other was connected with a clinic in Oregon (O Agency). Both agencies were located in central business districts in Beijing. Members of staff at both C Agency and O Agency invited me to visit their offices and attend some of their promotional events. During my visits, I was interested in learning more about how they approached potential clients and presented different fertility services. I interviewed members of staff, focusing on what they thought about the risks and success rates of fertility treatment and current regulations.

I visited advocacy groups, for they could provide me with an alternative interpretation of the regulations. I visited a feminist salon in Beijing where they discussed issues relating to reproduction among single women. Through attending the salon, I interviewed 4 single women who planned to freeze eggs (some in overseas clinics), 2 elective heterosexual single mothers, and 4 homosexual mothers who conceived children in overseas clinics with donated sperm. Some of these women were dealing with clinicians and officials as part of the process of applying for birth permission certificates and registering children in their households. In hearing about these interactions, I got a fresh perspective on how officials viewed the relationship between marriage and fertility treatment.

Mapping the chapters

In this chapter, I have introduced a series of conflicting discourses regarding the promotion and limitation of ARTs in China. At one level, ARTs are power technologies that align with the modernization goals of the Deng era. At another level, however, it raises numerous concerns, and the current regulations set up controversial criteria on the medicalization of ARTs, patients' marital status, and doctor-patient relationship. The main theme of this book, uncertainty, as articulated by my interviewees, explains why ARTs are restricted in China. According to them, ARTs embodied various forms of uncertainty, such as uncertain results, paternal uncertainty, and uncertain treatment plans. I have traced this theme of uncertainty in the context of Chinese modernization, where it informs reflections on Chairman Deng's modernization strategies, suggesting that some strategies should be reversed. I have introduced a term called spiral modernization to describe reversals and continuities in the Chinese modernization path. I have also described my approach to the ethnography in Beijing. My ethnography encompasses multiple sites, including clinics, regulatory bodies, fertility agencies, and a feminist salon.

When I discussed the current ARTs regulations with friends and members of my family, they always asked me why the government only allows it for medical purposes or why it has prohibited single women from having access to ARTs. The rationale behind these regulations is indeed puzzling. In an attempt to address the research vacuum surrounding this problem, in this book, I empirically analyze policy-making related to ARTs in China. Making sense of the regulations has not been easy because it was impossible for me to interview the policymakers who first drafted the regulations in 2003. In addition, the regulations are ambiguous at both national and local levels, with many competing narratives circulating in the public domain. I take the criteria of marriage as an example. If the government assumes that reproduction must take place within marriage, why does it allow single men to freeze sperm? There is also the conundrum of Jilin Province, where the more permissive policy clearly conflicts with national statutes that do not allow single women to use fertility treatment. How is it that, despite this clash, legislation in Jilin Province has remained unchanged since 2002?

This book addresses all of these questions. Rather than advance a judgment as to how ARTs should be regulated, I have tried to understand how policies are entwined with marriage, singledom, nationalism, social development, and politics by exploring diverse (and sometimes conflicted) narratives of clinicians, policymakers, patients, and activists. In so doing, I use ARTs as a lens through which to look at broader social changes in China. I show how discourses around ARTs are bound up with titanic battles between tradition and modernity, Eastern and Western ideologies, and socialism and capitalism during the modernization of Chinese society. This book explicates my original contribution to knowledge about ARTs policies in China and provides a nuanced understanding of contemporary Chinese society.

Chapter 2 will establish the historical contexts of Chinese spiral development. First, I will specify the negative consequences of Chairman Deng's modernization policies on technology development, population improvement, social open-up, free market, and political restructuring. These consequences shed light on my interviewees' concerns about ARTs. Then, I will present how political leaders address these consequences by repackaging traditional Chinese culture and tightening political control. These two policy reversals contextualize how my interviewees interpreted ARTs regulations in China. Finally, tracing the intellectual development of dialectics in Chinese history, I will introduce the spiral modernization path in China: although China continues to industrialize, urbanize, and open up its economy, many policies are reversed.

Chapters 3, 4, and 5 will explain the rationale behind the medicalization, marriage, and doctor-patient relationship criteria, exploring various forms of uncertainty surrounding ARTs. They will also show how reproductive uncertainty informs reflections and reversals of Chairman Deng's modernization policies.

In Chapter 3, I will explore why the regulations only allow medical use of ARTs. I will analyze how some interviewees, including clinicians and some patients, interpreted the term "success rates." They perceived success indicators, such as pregnancy rates or live birth rates, only pertained to particular variables (women who could achieve pregnancy or babies who could be born) at one given point in time. Regardless of the statistics, there was no guarantee that children would be born healthy and miscarriages would be averted. This uncertainty pertained to each stage of fertility treatment, from implantation to live birth, challenging the perceived omnipotence of modern technologies. I will also demonstrate how my interviewees repackaged the traditional Chinese beliefs of *Ming, Baoying,* and *zi ran* to describe this uncertainty. The traditional beliefs cautioned against excessive control over reproduction. Drawing from these beliefs, my interviewees reflected upon policies related to technology development, urbanization, and late childbearing.

Chapter 4 will focus on why the regulations emphasize patients' (especially women's) marital status in accessing ARTs. This chapter will revisit a traditional concept called paternal uncertainty. On one hand, in ancient societies, before the invention of DNA paternity tests, men were often uncertain if children were genetically related to them. Marrying virgin women was one strategy to protect men's genetic relationship with children. I show how single women who were supposed to be virgins, according to my interviewees, would "lose" their virginity if they used ARTs. Developing the evolutionary idea of "paternal uncertainty," my interviewees commented on pre-marital sex and social open-up in China. On the other hand, paternal uncertainty was rooted in traditional Confucian thoughts. Confucianism views births out of wedlock as shameful and illegitimate. I will analyze the ways in which single motherhood gives rise to paternal uncertainty. My interviewees were concerned about the rise of new family forms, such as single motherhood, during social open-up.

In Chapter 5, I will address a crisis in trust whereby fertility treatment in China becomes a powder keg. According to Ulrich Beck (1992), doctors and officials represent modern society's so-called "knowledge authorities" and, as such, are able to tackle risks. He argues that laypeople are becoming increasingly dependent on these authorities for their comprehension of the risks associated with technology and science. However, some interviewees in this ethnography viewed clinicians and government agencies as disengaged, irresponsible, and unprofessional. They saw them as sources of uncertainty. I will show how the government tightens political control in the face of ordinary people's distrust.

The final chapter will return to this book's overarching question: how do we understand restrictions of ARTs in the context of China's national development? This book makes sense of controversial ARTs regulations in China through continuities and reversals of modernization policies. I try to avoid a legalistic account that discusses whether these regulations deprive people of reproduction autonomy. However, I argue the government's connection of ARTs regulations with broader social changes in China politicizes individuals' fertility issues. Though some regulations are implemented in the name of protection, the government ensures individuals' reproduction (especially women's) aligns with policy agendas.

I hope this book will help readers understand not only the regulations of ARTs but also policy reversals and continuities in Chinese society. After decades of impressive growth, China has approached a crossroads involving both confusion and potential. As China is faced with a shrinking population and a long-term economic slowdown, I have heard prevailing skepticism over China's growth potential. I have also witnessed several policy reversals since I began research for this book in 2015. To halt the reduction in the birth rate, for example, the government replaced the One-Child Policy with the Two-Children Policy in 2016 and the Three-Children Policy in 2021. It rescinded the benefits accorded to those who marry late. Political leaders have also reinforced traditional values such as filial piety and Confucianism to encourage young people to conceive children. This book sets out to document and interpret some of these policy reversals. If successful, we will catch a glimpse of where Chinese modernization is heading.

Chapter 2

Reflection, Reversals, and Continuities

The world works in a spiral dynamic. The whole is an overcoming which preserves what it overcomes.
—Georg Wilhelm Friedrich Hegel, *Lectures on History of Philosophy*

Lessons learned

To evolve into a modern society and catch up with advanced Western countries, Chairman Deng revamped policies on technology, economy, population, and ideology. This book shows how contemporary social dynamics surrounding ARTs reflect concerns about the modernization strategies put forward by Chairman Deng. These concerns include over-reliance on science and technology, flexible kinship, commercialism, and the political crisis of authoritarianism. This chapter provides the historical background of the path of Chinese modernization. In this section, I specify the different stages of Chinese modernization in technology, demography, ideology, and economy from the late Qing Dynasty to the Deng era. I also elaborate on the negative consequences of Chairman Deng's modernization strategies.

Abuse of science and technology

Scientific and technological development is critical to Chinese society's long-term progress. For Qing Dynasty intellectuals, Western technologies such as firearms and the steam engine were framed as panaceas for China's social ills. For instance, a high-minded intellectual named Wei Yuan, who lived during the late Qing Dynasty, compiled a book titled An Illustrated Gazetteer of Maritime Countries (*hai tu guo zhi*). In it, he suggested that Chinese people should emulate Western technologies in order to resist Western invasions (*shi yi chang ji yi zhi yi*).

After founding the People's Republic of China in 1949, Chairman Mao aimed to catch up rapidly (*chao ying gan mei*) with Europe and the United States in terms of technology development in a socialist/communist way (Luo, 1993). His Great Leap Forward (*da yue jin*) campaign, for example, sought to incite technological development in a short space of time by means of radical industrialization and collectivization. The campaign mobilized the uneducated masses for research work and lowered professional standards for scientific and technical personnel. Many experts criticized the campaign; Chairman Mao branded them capitalist enemies. As such, they were sent to reeducation camps in rural areas to learn socialist principles. The Great Leap Forward and later the Cultural Revolution (*wen hua da ge ming*) represented the victory of anti-intellectualism and the devaluation of scientific scholarship, formal education, and professionalism in scientific research.

After the shadow of the Cultural Revolution dissipated, Chairman Deng's new reform-oriented government realized that China's technological products were poor and that there was a serious shortage of scientific personnel. Since 1983, therefore, the government has initiated national scientific and technological breakthrough plans. These have involved importing technologies, sending Chinese scientists abroad, building high-tech parks across the country, promoting innovation among state-owned firms, and guaranteeing intellectual property (Zhang, 1992). In addition, starting in 1986, the government began funding scientific and technological projects to promote domestic technology innovation. Indeed, there were many achievements in science and technology during Chairman Deng's leadership. ARTs represented significant achievements. Other achievements included satellite-recovering technology, missiles from underwater, and high-density information storage research. All of these achievements underscored China's global prominence in fields such as atomic energy, aerospace engineering, high-energy physics, bio-medicine, and computer science.

However, concerns over the abuse of technology such as data mining, AI-powered surveillance, facial recognition, and human gene editing have loomed in China in the recent decade. Perhaps one of the most shocking cases of technology abuse in China after I began the ethnography is the Clustered Regularly Interspaced Short Palindromic Repeats (CRISPER) babies scandal. On November 26, 2018, Chinese scientist Jianqui announced that he successfully produced the world's first gene-edited babies who were genetically resistant to AIDS. Though gene editing could inadvertently alter genes in unpredictable ways, the study is still completed with governmental support. According to the study's clinical trial registration, which was still accessible online (CHICTR, 2018), the source of funding was from Shenzhen Science and Technology Innovation Free Exploration Project of the Shen Zhen Technology Innovation Committee, a government office. Shenzhen Science and Technology Innovation Free Exploration Project responds to the government's call for massive investment in technology.

This scandal urged the Chinese government to increasingly reflect upon the excessive use of technologies. As the government acknowledged after the scandal, "China lacks a rigorous regulation and supervision mechanism for evaluating ethics in scientific research and technological development"

(ChinaDaily, 2019). To supervise science and technology development, in 2019, the ninth meeting of the Central Committee for Deepening Overall Reform (*zhong yang quan mian shen hua gai ge wei yuan hui*) passed Plan on Establishing a National Science and Technology Ethics Committee (Xinhua, 2019).

Technology development mechanizes productive forces, fueling urbanization. China's urbanization was indeed dramatic. The share of population in cities in the total population of a country was only 10.64% in 1949. Nevertheless, in 2019, it reached around 60.31%. Hundreds of Chinese cities of all sizes competed to look modernized, building Manhattanesque skylines and multi-lane highways (Yeh and Xu, 2009). People replaced swathes of fertile, well-irrigated agricultural land and other natural resources with factories and high-rises (He, Huo, and Zhang, 2002).

This massive exploitation of nature brings adverse effects. The traffic congestion in front of the P Clinic, for example, represents a typical ailment of modern urban life. The road was under construction during my fieldwork. Dust swirled around me as I walked along it every morning. On both sides of the road, buildings were veiled in dust. Since March 2014, it has been the site of roadworks, which aimed to broaden the four-lane road, thus alleviating congestion. Although the construction works were scheduled to end in September 2014, they continued into 2016. Ironically, the roadworks increased traffic. Vehicles moved forward so slowly that the road almost resembled a car park. The congestion was one manifestation of a congested and polluted industrial megapolis created by Beijing's rapid growth.

The government now pays more attention to the environmental consequences of urbanization. For example, Chairman Xi Jinping formulated the Two Mountain Theory and developed a slogan called "clear waters and green mountains are as valuable as gold and silver mountains" (*lv shui qing shan jiu shi jin shan yin shan*).[1] His slogan emphasizes the importance of the natural environment in national development.

Fertility decline

Besides technological development, attempts to improve population quality have also formed another crucial part of China's modernization strategies. In the late Qing dynasty, the notion of eugenics was introduced in China, which

---

[1] Chairman Jinping Xi was the current General Secretary of the Chinese Communist Party, President of the People's Republic of China, and Chairman of the Central Military Commission. He has been a prominent figure in contemporary Chinese politics since assuming power in 2012.

shed new light on demographic management. Chinese reformers tried to steer clear of notions of racism and colonialism. On the one hand, they promoted a policy of increasing the number of genetically desirable people over the idea that genetically undesirable people should be eliminated. For example, Guangdan Pan, who introduced the basic principles of eugenics (1995) in China, encouraged educated and intelligent Chinese people to conceive more children. On the other hand, Chinese eugenics programs paid attention to the importance of nurture and environment rather than focusing solely on race and genes. During the Republican Era, government education and health programs cared for sick, pregnant women so as to create a healthy and robust citizenry from the moment of conception onward.

When the Communist Party took power, eugenics was harshly criticized on account of their inherent class bias. Though the New Marriage Law, which was implemented in 1950, mentioned that people with certain diseases were unfit for marriage, Chairman Mao's natalist policies encouraged women to conceive as many children as possible so as to increase the labor force. Women were awarded the title of Mother Heroine for bearing and raising large families. During the Cultural Revolution, Eugenicists such as Guangdan Pan and Chongrui Yang were denounced as counter-revolutionaries.

Unlike Chairman Mao, Chairman Deng viewed rapid population growth as an encumbrance, not a resource. Accordingly, he promoted the One-Child Policy. The One-Child policy was criticized by scholars and human rights groups for its harsh local enforcement. Those who followed the policy could receive financial incentives and employment opportunities, while those who did not abide by the policy had to pay fines and even experienced forced sterilizations and abortions (Pletcher 2015). However, this was one of the most important modernization policies attempted under Chairman Deng's leadership. As Susan Greenhalgh has written, they "represent an extraordinary attempt to engineer national wealth, power, and global standing by drastically breaking population growth" (2003, p.163).

In addition to barbaric measures of controlling women's fertility, the government promoted an incentive called Late Marriage and Late Childbearing. People who postpone marriage and childbearing age can receive holiday benefits. The rationale behind the incentive for this policy was that late marriage and childbearing prolong the cycle by which a population replaces itself, which makes it easier to control total population growth (Wu, 1997).

Indeed, the age at which Chinese youth get married or have children has increased steadily in the past 30 years. According to the National Bureau of Statistics (1990, 2000, 2010, 2020), in 2020, the average age for first marriages stood at 28.67 years, marking an increase of 5.89 years from 22.78 years in 1990. Women's childbearing age has increased from 23.49 in 1995 to 27.64 in 2020.

The rate of single population between 25 and 29 also increased significantly. The rate of increasing in singledom among women has increased more quickly than among men, though men are still more likely to be single. In 1995, 18.2% of men and 5.5% of women in this age bracket were single; in 2020, 55.6% of men and 39% of women between 25 and 29 were single.

One of the reasons why Late Marriage and Late Childbearing influence more women than men is because this incentive allows women to thrive in areas they did not have access to before and come closer to social equality with men (Goeking, 2019). It was hoped that women would complete nine years of compulsory education and find paid jobs instead of becoming homemakers. Consequently, female participation in the labor force has increased since 1980. China has one of the highest female employment rates in the Asia-Pacific region (Asian Development Bank, 2017).[2] What is more, China has achieved gender parity in schooling. According to data from the United Nations Educational, Scientific and Cultural Organization (UNESCO) (2019a; 2019b), the gender parity index of secondary and tertiary school enrollment in China has surpassed line one. This means that today, girls have greater access to schooling than boys. A study of gender parity in college enrollment undertaken by sociologists Binzhen Wu and Xiaohan Zhong (2014) also indicates that in China, college is now just as accessible to women as it is to men.

Nevertheless, together with more education and career opportunities, a plethora of social and structural factors "force" more women than men into staying single or not conceiving children. Here, I name a few factors. First, the so-called "marriage gradient" in Chinese society makes it practically impossible for women with careers or educational accomplishments to find compatible partners in the marriage market. The concept of the marriage gradient, developed by US sociologist Jessie Bernard (1982), refers to the male propensity to find female partners from lower social classes. When men increase in social status, they expand their pool of eligibles; when women increase in social status, they narrow their pool of eligibles, exacerbating the female marriage squeeze. In China, the better-paid and educated women become, the fewer choices they have on the marriage market. According to Tianhui Gui's (2016) study of matchmaking events held in four parks in Beijing, women's education and income were less valued than their age and appearance.

---

[2] Women's labor force participation rate has shown a downward trend since the 1990s, decreasing from 79% in 1990 to 71% in 2019 (World Bank, 2024). The reasons for this decline include improvements in unemployment insurance, occupational discrimination against women, and increasing childcare costs, among others (Xi, 2017a).

Second, women postpone marriage or childbearing because they struggle to balance work and family. Although Chinese laws ban gender discrimination in the workplace, they do not clearly define what constitutes gender discrimination. Consequently, they provide few effective enforcement mechanisms, and gender-based employment discrimination is still common. "Chinese employers frequently discriminate on gender grounds, both directly and indirectly" (Woodhams et al., 2009, p.2084). Women were asked about their plans for marriage and pregnancy during job interviews; some had their job applications rejected because they were soon to get married (Wang and Klugman, 2020). These recruitment practices reflect "highly segregated expectations of men and women's roles at work [which] hinder women's progress in the labor market" (Woodhams et al., 2009, p.2084). To increase their opportunities for finding jobs and advancing their careers, female employees tend to postpone childbearing and work harder than men.

Third, given that the burden of housework and childcare is still largely placed on women, some women are concerned that they may have to quit their jobs to take care of their families once they get married and/or have children (Choi, 2008; Foster and Ren 2014; Zhou et al., 2018). Work units (*dan wei*), which provided childcare, nursing rooms for breastfeeding, and paid maternity leave, were dissolved in the Deng era, making way for privatization. Cook and Dong (2014) have suggested that the privatization and commercialization of childcare services have added to women's domestic responsibilities, limiting their occupational choices and autonomy.

Late Marriage and Late Childbearing speed up the decline of the total fertility rate. The total fertility rate (TFR) dropped from 5.81 in 1970 to 2.75 in 1979; it dropped to below 2.1 in the 1990s (Jiang et al, 2019). The TFRs recorded in the 2010 and 2020 censuses were 1.18 and 1.30, respectively (National Bureau of Statistics, 2010; National Bureau of Statistics, 2020). China's National Bureau of Statistics reported annual births of 10.62 million in 2021 (Wang, 2022). The annual births were 9.56 million in 2022, a sharp decline of 9.98% compared to the births in 2021 (National Bureau of Statistics, 2023).

The government is concerned that the fertility decline will rapidly accelerate the aging process in China, fueling the risk of rising labor costs, reduced competitiveness, and an overburdened social welfare system. As Chairman Xi said at the meeting of the Political Bureau of the Central Committee on May 31, 2021, "Nowadays, population issue has been a strategic issue. We need to coordinate the promotion of childbirth policies with related economic and social policies" (NPC, 2021). Following Chairman Xi's speech, on the same day, the Political Bureau of the Central Committee approved the "Decision of the Central Committee of the Communist Party of China and the State Council on Optimizing Fertility Policies to Promote Long-term Balanced Population

Development" (the Decision) which proposed to amend the Population and Family Planning Law, promote marriage and childbearing at the right age and implement the Three-Children Policy. The Decision especially criticizes Late Marriage and Late Childbearing which has become an important factor affecting the level of fertility in China. According to the Decision, delaying the age of marriage and childbearing will compress the best time for women to give birth, reducing the possibility of multiple births.

Social open-up

To end colonial exploitation, from the late Qing dynasty to the Republic era, reformers welcomed Western cultures in order to achieve a complete overhaul of Chinese society. The May Fourth Movement, for example, witnessed a surge of interest in a variety of ideologies, such as science and democracy, from the outside world.

However, after founding the People's Republic of China, Chairman Mao launched a few campaigns to ensure Western culture did not dilute people's revolutionary ideas. For example, during the Cultural Revolution, most foreign films were rejected (Li, 2023). Libraries of foreign texts were destroyed, and scholars who used to study abroad were labeled "anti-party element" (*fan dang fen zi*) and sent to rural labor camps.

Chairman Deng rejected the theoretical underpinnings of the "Great Cultural Revolution" and ushered in a new era of cultural openness. He encouraged China's cultural, educational, and professional exchanges with foreign countries. Inevitably, ideas such as individualism, liberalism, democracy, and feminism began to influence Chinese people.

One consequence is the dramatic change in Chinese people's attitudes toward sex (Xiao, Mehrotra, and Zimmerman, 2011). According to sociologist Suiming Pan's description of Chinese sexuality history, "the Open and Reform Policy is the father, and the One-Child Policy is the mother of China's current revolution in sexual mores and behaviors" (2006, p.31). On the one hand, the opening up of Chinese society has changed people's perception of sexuality, which emphasizes personal pleasure over reproduction goals. As sociologist Amy Braverman (2002) notes, the Western sexual culture was also introduced in China when China opened up to the global economy in the early 1980s.[3] Consequently, when Chinese young people are in intimate relationships, they focus on pleasure rather than the path toward marriage (Yang, 2011). Second,

---

[3] Triggered by the development of contraception pills and the women's suffrage movement, the Western sexual revolution occurred in the twentieth century. It reached a climax in the 1960s. It promoted social acceptance of homosexuality and premarital sex.

especially for women, the introduction of the One-Child Policy serves to separate sex from reproduction. "Women have gradually begun to reject their traditional role as either asexual beings existing only for reproduction and childbearing or the passive sexual objects of male demands" (Zhang and Beck, 1999, p.107). Increasingly, women are paying attention to the pleasure of sex (Pan, 2006).

Since China's "sexual opening-up" (*xing kai fang*) in the 1980s, young people's attitudes toward pre-marital sex have become liberal. Sociologist Suiming Pan's comparison of college students' sex practices in 2001 with those in 2006 reveals that the rate of premarital sexual intercourse has almost doubled, increasing from 16.9% to 32% respectively (2017). A study conducted among 54,580 college students from 1,764 higher education institutions spanning 34 provinces in China, as well as Hong Kong, Macao, and Taiwan, has similar findings (Statista, 2020). Approximately 64.6 percent of survey participants expressed acceptance of premarital sex.

Another consequence of China's opening up is the significant endorsement of individualism and a growing emphasis on personal well-being among young people (Yu, 1997; Bai, 1998). Familialism is less important among younger generations. For example, sociologists Jiaming Sun and Xun Wang have assessed differences in the values held across four generations of residents of Shanghai, one of the most modernized parts of China (2010). Although family allegiances have remained central across the examined age groups, younger generations were more likely to prioritize nuclear families and less likely to emphasize family clans than their older equivalents. Moreover, nontraditional families (such as single parenthood and childless families) are increasingly popular as many young people are unwilling to marry or conceive children.

Collectivism and nationalism also faded after China's Open and Reform. Sociologists Liza Steele and Scott Lynch's study of Chinese people's subjective well-being between 1990 and 2007 indicates that national pride has become less important among young Chinese people (2013). Political leaders are very concerned that the state and society might gradually lose coherence. In his speech to China's youth during the celebration of the May Fourth Movement, Chairman Xi appealed to young people to be "grateful to the party, country, society, and people" (Xi, 2018). He warned against the wholesale imitation of Western liberal democracy. As he put it, young people should "consciously resist mistaken thoughts such as the worship of money, hedonism, extreme individualism, and historical nihilism" (Xi, 2018).

Marketization of healthcare

Upon assuming power in 1949, the Chinese Communist Party's primary goal was to transform China into a modern and powerful nation. Economically, this entails industrialization, poverty alleviation, and improvement of people's living standards. During the Mao era, China's economy was largely demonetized and decommodified. The government encouraged and later forced private business owners to either sell their businesses to the state or transform their businesses into joint ventures with the state. However, these initiatives for the public economy ended in economic catastrophe, resulting in a great famine between 1959 and 1961, during which an estimated thirty million people died.

In 1978, Chairman Deng changed this public economy policy, seeking to salvage the failing economy by opening up to the global market. His approach to the market economy included the decollectivization of agriculture, openness to foreign investment, granting entrepreneurs permission to establish businesses, privatizing and outsourcing many state-owned industries, and fostering collaboration between private and state industries.

As the government reoriented the country's centrally planned economy toward the market, a majority of health institutions were no longer owned and operated by the government. The government cut hospitals' funding, forcing them to find ways of sustaining themselves independently. Many public hospitals, therefore, depend on profits from drug sales and diagnostic tests (Li et al., 2012; Yi et al., 2015). The three-tier system of healthcare access, established during the Mao era, gradually collapsed. The first tier consisted of so-called barefoot doctors (*chi jiao yi sheng*) who were equipped with basic knowledge of medicine. The second tier comprised small outpatient clinics (such as township health centers), while the third tier consisted of county/city hospitals for seriously ill patients. Due to a shortage of state funding, well-resourced, hospital-based specialty care proliferated in cities, while barefoot doctors, receiving little government support, ceased practicing.

The marketization of healthcare has led to increased healthcare costs. The general public could no longer receive essential health services for free. Additionally, given the unequal distribution of health resources among regions (Zhou et al., 2015), patients tend to crowd into top-ranked urban clinics (Daemmrich, 2013) and reduce visits to community-level clinics (Wu and Lam, 2016). As a consequence of deficiencies in the healthcare system reform, the relationship between patients and doctors becomes tense. The government, acknowledging the pitfalls of a free market, especially the commercialization of Medicare, is now cautious. In one of Chairman Xi's speeches at an annual legislative session, he stated, "We've come to the understanding that we should not ignore the blindness of the market" (Quoted in People's Daily, 2019).

Chairman Xi emphasized the need to avoid full commercialization of healthcare to protect public welfare.

Social conflicts

Following the market economy is political reform. To kick off the marketization of the economy, Chairman Deng called for changes in how China was governed. He refined the unitary system that emphasizes political centralization (Zhu, 2003). He adopted a principal-agent relationship, whereby one person or body (the "agent") acts in the name of another (the "principal"). CCP committees are principals, whereas government officials are agents. Party leaders propose directions for reform; government officials take action to release these plans. The principal-agent relationship offers local officials flexibility in implementing policies. Officials are promoted for remarkable achievements (Zhang, 1997).

The principal-agent relationship relieves the party's burden of constantly intervening in policy-making and incentivizes officials to design suitable action plans. However, it also has side effects. Officials' inaction is one of the side effects. On the one hand, as officials act according to their own interests, they can overlook public services that do not contribute to their own work or further their hopes for promotion. On the other hand, as superiors do not provide clear instructions on how to implement policies in order not to make mistakes, subaltern officials prefer to wait for clearer instructions rather than take immediate action.

How local officials behave can often have immediate and tangible impacts on people's everyday lives. Poor bureaucratic practices occasion a sense of estrangement between ordinary people and officials, sparking an outpouring of anger and distrust. The White Paper Movement (*bai zhi yun dong*), during which Chinese people occupied streets and displayed blank A4 papers to protest against officials' COVID quarantine measures, is perhaps the biggest protest against the government in the recent decade. Concerned about the increasingly tense relationship between ordinary people and officials, Chairman Xi said, "There are still many conflicts that influence social stability. Some historical problems are unresolved, and the pressure of development has brought new conflicts" (quoted in Ma, 2017). The intensive social conflicts have provided legitimacy for activists to call for political reform. The government did not welcome activism in ending conflicts. As Chairman Xi warned, "Some interest groups utilize the internet as main contact channels, leading to activism both online and offline. Activism poses potential challenges to [social stability]" (quoted in Ma, 2017).

The New Era (*xin shi dai*)

Political leaders' concerns about Chairman Deng's modernization policies include abuse of technology, fertility decline, liberalism, commercialism, and social conflicts. They worry that China will have to pay a heavy social price for its rapid development. These costs might ultimately derail China's upward trajectory, leaving the government unable to retain its legitimacy simply by referring to its economic achievements. Now, I introduce how political leaders refine Chairman Deng's policies.

Chairman Xi brands his response to Chairman Deng's modernization policies as the New Era (*xin shi dai*) rather than "modernization," perhaps to differentiate his policies from Chairman Deng's. According to his explanation of the New Era at the 19th National Congress of the communist party of China in 2017,

> As socialism with Chinese characteristics has entered a new era, the principal contradiction facing Chinese society has evolved. What we now face is the contradiction between unbalanced and inadequate development, and the people's ever-growing need for a better life (Xi, 2017b).

Chairman Xi realized that previous modernization policies had brought challenges, namely unbalanced and inadequate development. According to him, the New Era tackles these challenges and sets up new development goals. He urged the government to achieve common prosperity for everyone after China transformed from a poor country into a relatively prosperous one.

The two key measures that Chairman Xi and his administration take in response to issues such as abuse of technology, fertility decline, and commercialism are repackaging traditional Chinese culture and reinforcing political control. Both measures are reversals of what Chairman Deng recommended. However, Chairman Xi has not pursued an overhaul of Chairman Deng's modernization policies. He raised a slogan called Two Unwaverings (*liang ge bu dong yao*). Two Unwaverings mean policies and policy reversals could co-exist. He illustrated Two Unwaverings with his stance on market economy, for example. He supported the market economy but also emphasized the importance of the public economy.

In this section, I explain in detail how Chairman Xi's government dealt with the challenges of Chairman Deng's modernization policies with four policy cases: namely, Chinese Characteristics for a New Era, Outlook of Family in New Era, Harmonious Society, and Two Establishes and Two Safeguards. The first three cases show how the government repackages traditional Chinese culture to prevent issues such as technology abuse and fertility decline, and the last case shows how the government reinforces political control to avoid social conflicts.

Chinese Characteristics for the New Era

The phrase Chinese Characteristics for the New Era (*zhong guo te se de xin shi dai*) was initially formulated by Chairman Xi, who proposed that China should develop an alternative to the Western model. In this way, Chairman Xi expects that China will become a leading global power by the middle of the twenty-first century. The alternative, according to Chairman Xi, is rejuvenating tradition. Chairman Xi has declared "traditional thought cultures the soul of the nation" (Xinhua, 2016). He has called for more education in traditional culture among young Chinese people, characterizing the endeavor as a "soul-forging project" (*zhu hun gong cheng*) (quoted in Wang, 2017). Tradition provides a vantage point from which to reassess past modernization policies and thus inspire future practice. As Chairman Xi has said:

> Outstanding traditional culture is the basis of a country and nation's continuation and development. Losing it is the same as severing a country and nation's lifeline. … A nation's power and prosperity must always be supported by a flourishing culture. The prosperous development of Chinese culture is the prerequisite for the great rejuvenation of the Chinese nation (Quoted in Xue 2017).

For Chairman Xi, rejuvenating tradition does not mean relinquishing development. Instead, he pursues modernization alongside the attempted creation of a new, unique Chinese identity by the revival of tradition.

Rather than becoming a source of social ills, tradition could cure social problems. Chairman Xi suggests that Chinese scientists embrace traditional Chinese culture in order to avoid abuse of technology. According to him, traditional Chinese culture pays attention to ethics and morality, which is meaningful during the development of science and technology (2021). He emphasized that scientists should consider the technological impact on society. Chinese traditional culture, which values nature and sustainable development, helps scientists to develop technology ethically.

Political leaders also believe that tradition could prevent the Westernization of Chinese society as it opens up. On the one hand, tradition legitimizes rhetoric proclaiming China's unique way of development. As Chairman Xi has said, "China's unique cultural tradition and unique historical condition have determined that China must follow the road of development that fits Chinese characteristics" (quoted in Foreign Ministry of the People's Republic of China,

2014). He insists that the Western brand of modernization is not the only possible form of development: modernization and Westernization are not synonymous. Celebrating the 100th anniversary of the May Fourth Movement, which marked the beginning of Chinese modernization, Chairman Xi (2014) stressed that "we cannot forget our ancestors and cannot copy the development models of foreign countries. Nor can we accept any instructions imposed by foreigners."

On the other hand, tradition could instill confidence in China's unique development. This is particularly clear in economist Weiwei Zhang's book named *The China Wave: Rise of a Civilizational State*, which has been endorsed by top party leaders, notably Chairman Xi. Zhang's book argues that Chinese people should be proud of their traditions. "China is the only nation," Zhang explains,

> where a millennia-old civilization fully coincides with the morphology of a modern state. ... It is as though ancient Rome was never dissolved, and continued to the present day, making the transition to a modern nation-state, with a central government and a modern economy, incorporating traditional cultural elements, having a massive population in which everyone speaks Latin. (2012, p.21.)

Zhang regards China as the only nation in the world that is able to incorporate traditional culture completely into the framework of modernization. This uniqueness reinforces cultural confidence. For example, during his visit to Macao in 2014, Chairman Xi emphasized that cultural confidence is the basis of China's efforts to rejuvenate itself (Quoted in Liang, 2019). He referred to the example of traditional Chinese medicine, presenting it as great because it can still be used today.

Outlook of Family in the New Era

The Outlook of Family in the New Era is proposed by Chairman Xi to address fertility decline and social open-up. He emphasizes "the family, family education, and family values" (*zhu zhong jia ting, zhu zhong jia jiao, zhu zhong jiafeng*) (ChinaDaily, 2018). For Chairman Xi, the family is the spiritual and moral foundation of Chinese civilization. In his speech at the 2015 Spring Festival group meeting, Chairman Xi quoted the poem Song of the Wanderer (*you zi yin*) by Tang Dynasty poet Meng Jiao to demonstrate the importance of family in Chinese society.

Several traditional family perceptions inform the Outlook of Family in the New Era. According to Chairman Xi,

The traditional Chinese culture is family-oriented, which is significantly different from the individual-oriented culture in the West. Chinese people regard family as the starting point and destination of life and regard raising children, self-cultivation, and governing the country and world as life goals. (2015).

For Chairman Xi, individuals in contemporary society should follow traditional Chinese culture and view the family as the starting point of life. He particularly emphasizes that raising children should be a priority. In other words, he does not support placing career goals or other personal development goals ahead of building a family.

The Outlook of Family in the New Era is part of pro-natal policies. To avert plummeting birth rates and marriage rates, Chairman Xi's government introduced the Three-Children Policy and canceled the benefits accorded to those who marry late. While the Three-Children Policy targets the entire population, the Outlook of Family in the New Era specifically focuses on women's familial roles. It reaffirms that women should prioritize families over careers. As an example of a virtuous woman, Chairman Xi cited Mother Meng's devotion to her son (An, 2018). Mother Meng, the mother of Mencius, was a renowned historical figure who moved her family three times in pursuit of a better education for her son. This story underscores mothers' sacrifices for their children's futures. When Chairman Xi referenced Mother Meng's story, his message was clear: a virtuous woman prioritizes her family and children's interests over her own. He implied that women should dedicate themselves to conceiving children early in life and caring for their families rather than pursuing personal goals. An Amendment to the Women's Rights and Interests Protection Law passed by the People's Congress reflects the Outlook of Family in the New Era. The amendment introduced a few moral standards for women to adhere to. "Women should respect and obey national laws, respect social morals, professional ethics, and family values" (Xiao, 2022), according to the law's introduction chapter, which outlines the fundamental principles of the revised legislation. The amendment molds women's intimate lives to conform to patriarchal norms.

In addition to emphasizing women's family responsibilities, the Outlook of Family in the New Era promotes the preference for virgin brides. China Women's Daily (2017), an official newspaper issued by the Women's Federation, once promoted courses for Good Women in the New Era. These courses instilled traditional cultural values regarding virginity in women. These courses reflect policymakers' belief that sex should only occur within marriage in the New Era. This conservative norm of sexual morality cautions against the increasingly liberal attitudes toward sex during China's social open-up.

The Outlook of Family in the New Era also asserts that a perfect family has a husband as its head, supported by a virtuous wife. According to the government's perspective, single motherhood does not align with this traditional family model. Chairman Xi views this family model as the foundation of Chinese society. He believes that "the family model is not only the essence of traditional Chinese families but also the concrete manifestation of socialist core values, modern marriage, family laws, and moral norms" (2016).

Harmonious Society

As a response to the increasing alleged social injustice and inequality emerging in Chinese society, Chairman Hu Jintao proposed a Harmonious Society (*he xie she hui*).[4] For Chairman Hu, harmony means the interests of different social sectors are balanced. Hu's successor, Chairman Xi (2013), also incorporated the notion of social balance into his policies, which projects a peaceful domestic society and promotes "peace, development, cooperation, and win-win relations" in global systems.

The concept of social harmony derives from the idea of interrelation, a dialectical argument developed in ancient Chinese philosophy. Traditional Chinese thought was structured around a series of tangible dualities—such as brightness and darkness, private and public, fragmentation and unity. These were seen as the physical manifestations of ostensibly opposed forces. In the natural world, however, these forces are actually complementary and interdependent. Indeed, one force may give rise to its opposite. Traditional philosophy regarded the world as harmonious because opposite forces are interrelated. The idea helps solve conflicts. Take the interrelationship among Confucianism, Daoism, and Buddhism as an example. They were the three main religions in traditional Chinese society. However, unlike many societies that turn religious differences into violence, such as the long history of persecution of Jews and the continuing conflicts between Muslim Pakistan and Hindu India, Chinese people believed these three religions were trilaterally complementary (*ru shi dao hu bu*). In this schema, Daoism portrays the root of the whole universe and the original substance of life; Buddhism describes spirituality and the afterlife; Confucianism addresses the original dispensation of moral and social value. As the Chinese philosopher Zehou Li put it, Daoism is the root, Buddhism is the stem, and Confucianism is the flower (Li, 1981).

Interrelation means individuals are not separate entities. They are connected with each other. A "balance of interests," therefore, not only incorporates

---

[4] Chairman Jintao Hu was General Secretary of the CCP between 2002 and 2012.

different stakeholders but also favors agreement among actors with divergent interests and values by claiming those interests and values are interrelated. Interests do not ultimately come into conflicts, the logic goes, because everyone is interrelated. Therefore, the question of how to cope with competing interests does not concern decision-makers. It need not be asked whose interests are the most important since all interests coexist harmoniously. This view is different from utilitarian perspectives of dealing with interest conflicts. According to Bentham and Charles (2009), the question of whether an action is right or wrong can be determined by reference to its consequences. Whereas righteous actions maximize pleasure, wrongful actions maximize pain. In making moral choices, policymakers should measure the pleasure and pain they expect a particular policy to bring about. In this way, when social interests are more important than individual rights, the government fulfills social interests and overlooks individual rights. The key narrative put forward in Harmonious Society, however, is that all parties' interests are interrelated with one another—not that simple calculations should lead policymakers to choose one route over another.

A clinician during my fieldwork raised a story about a single woman who had been born without a vagina to illustrate how a balance of interests could solve medical conflicts. This lady came to P Clinic and wanted to make an artificial vagina in secret so that she could find a husband. P Clinic declined her request due to her marital status, wanting to protect the interests of the lady's future husband. However, the clinician did not regard P Clinic as overlooking the lady's rights. She believed in the interrelationship between the lady's happiness and her future husband's satisfaction. The lady proceeded to undergo surgery in a private clinic. However, despite having an artificial vagina implanted, she felt so embarrassed about it that she did not get married. The clinician demonstrated that the lady should not be angry about P Clinic for declining her treatment request.

Two Establishes and Two Safeguards

To curtail dissent and political mobilization, political leaders closely coordinate state control of domestic activity. For example, Chairman Xi promoted a slogan called Two Establishes and Two Safeguards (*liang ge que li liang ge wei hu*). Two objectives are "To establish the status of Comrade Jinping Xi as the core of the Party's Central Committee and of the whole Party and to establish the guiding role of Jinping Xi Thought on Socialism with Chinese Characteristics for the New Era" (China Media Project, 2022). Two Safeguards are "to safeguard the 'core' status of Chairman Xi within the CCP and to safeguard the centralized authority of the Party"(China Media Project, 2022).

The slogan was added to the Party Constitution during the 20th National Congress of the CCP.

Two Establishes and Two Safeguards strengthen Xi's personal rule. It equates Xi's leadership with opposition to the Party itself. The last political leader who had such political influence was Chairman Mao. Chairman Xi appropriated the iconic power of Chairman Mao. For instance, Xi has attempted to demonstrate his courage, passion, and wisdom through elegiac songs posted on social media. Some of the titles of these songs include "Be A Man Like Xi if You Want to Be," "Marry A Man Like Xi if You Want to Marry," and "National People's Idol Xi." Much like Chairman Mao, Xi seeks to reinforce his authority by fostering a "personal, trusting, and infantilizing bond" (Glassman, 1976, p.630) between him and the public by promoting these songs.

Two Establishes and Two Safeguards also maximize the party's power. The party has more legitimacy to quash dissent. For example, when the "MeToo" movement peaked in China, police arrested some Chinese feminists who had made sexual allegations against their bosses and colleagues on social media. The party was worried that these feminists colluded with Western forces to overthrow its rule.

Chairman Xi's emphasis on political control can be understood as a response to the social unrest, widening regional disparities, and competing ideologies that have resulted from Chairman Deng's reforms. The more open the society, the tighter the political control needed to ensure its stability. The challenge that party leaders face is very straightforward: how can they sustain their legitimacy (which is based on the past achievements of China's modernization policies) amid the disadvantages caused by modernization? They aim to reshape the party's legitimacy, presenting the party itself as a source of solidarity. It follows from this that Chairman Xi should launch a cult of personality to recover popular support. In this way, it is hoped that the people will adhere to the party itself rather than just the economic growth it has brought about.

Spiral Society

So far, I have outlined the drawbacks of modernization policies advocated by Chairman Deng. I have also introduced that Chairman Xi rejuvenates traditional Chinese culture and tightens political control to deal with these challenges. Many theorists view tradition and political control as antithetical to modernity (Parsons, 1951; Lerner, 1958; Inkeles, 1969; Eisenstadt, 1984). For example, sociologist Talcott Parsons (1964) argues that culture and tradition indigenous to developing societies impede their economic growth. Seymour Martin Lipset (1959) claims abandonment of tradition is deemed worthwhile especially for less developed countries. He also believes democracy leads to development. As he has put it, "all the various aspects of economic development—industrialization, urbanization, wealth, and education—are so closely interrelated as to form one major factor which has the political correlate of democracy" (1963, p.41). Therefore, it seems that Chairman Xi has reversed modernization policies. However, he does not forsake the idea of modernization. According to him (2022), modernization with Chinese characteristics remains the primary goal during the New Era.

Chairman Xi creates a paradoxical development path: tradition and political centralization coexist with modernization. The coexistence challenges the linear narrative of social development and calls for alternative theories. Skepticism regarding progressive social development is not new. Eighty years ago, after the end of World War Two, many theorists questioned whether modernity represented the ultimate stage of social development. As Ulrich Beck has observed, technological advancement gave rise to warfare and ecological crises, and scientists lost their authority in the face of mass communication and globalization; the emergence of new non-governmental forces challenged the legitimacy of governments and states (1992). In these ways, the drawbacks of techno-scientific rationality backfired on modernity, challenging its very basis. This led to the emergence of a fresh debate about whether modernity had been superseded, which started in Europe and spread to America.

Post-modernists such as Jean-François Lyotard and Jean Baudrillard claim that the era of modernity had come to an end in the aftermath of the Second World War, ushering in a period they label post-modernity. During this era, many tenets of modernity were challenged. For example, science lost authority in its pursuit of truth after television became the primary information source (Lyotard, 1979). Rationality becomes highly contextualized, applying within specific cultural paradigms (Nye, 1990). Frustration and disillusionment over democracy grew as a small group of privileged elites, rather than the mass populace, came to manipulate political systems (Crouch, 2004).

On the contrary, late modernists such as Anthony Giddens and Ulrich Beck argue that modernity persisted in developed societies. They argue that the second half of the twentieth century represents not post-modernity but an alternative form of modernity. Beck, for example, introduced the concept of "reflexive modernity." Consider how sociologist Ulrich Beck, in his famous book *Risk Society: Towards a New Modernity*, described "the expansion of modernization risks—with the endangering of nature, health, nutrition and so on" (1992, p.36). For Beck, risks such as air pollution and climate change were generated by the development of science and technology in modern society. To cope with risks, "modernization," he writes, "is becoming reflexive" (1992, p.9).

Universal suffrage, the welfare state, and social movements are expressions of reflexive modernity.

In non-Western countries, after the Second World War, although many adopted Western-style modernization, not all sustained it, and even fewer succeeded. For example, despite receiving significant aid from the US government, both Chile and especially Argentina's progress toward modernization was suspended or reversed before the rule of Peron. Moreover, the relationship between democracy and modernization was challenged by the rise of militarism in Japan. As sociologist Shmuel Eisenstadt (1964) had written, "We witness the breakdown of a relatively differentiated and modern framework, the establishment of a less differentiated framework or the development of blockages and eruptions leading to institutionalized stagnation, rigidity, and instability" (p.382). Hence, theorists in non-western countries also seek to broaden the concept of modern development. Eisenstadt (2003) introduced the concept of "multiple modernities," suggesting that modernization paths are diverse and not exclusively tied to European or American culture. Whereas Shmuel Eisenstadt explained why societies adopt different strategies of modernization, Kyung-Sup Chang (2010) analyzed why indigenous culture persists in modernizing societies. He attributed it to the condensed nature of modernization in terms of both time and space, as observed in Korea.

Like postmodern and late-modern theories, the policy reversals proposed by Chairman Xi respond to challenges brought by modernization policies. However, Chairman Xi's approach neither rejects modernization nor advocates for modernity's self-reform. Beck suggests that in times of crisis, political control relaxes in the face of civil rights movements. In sharp contrast, China reverses rather than reforms modernization policies by tightening up political control. Also, although Kyung-Sup Chang's "compressed modernity" can explain the co-existence between modernization and tradition in Chinese society due to China's rapid pace of modernization, it does not explain why China deliberately reverses certain modernization policies at certain points. Reflecting on the continuities and reversals that characterize China's modernization path, then, it is clear that a new concept is needed.

From theory to history

What strategies for development are open to China beyond those promoted by Europe and the United States? I have introduced the concept of "spiral modernization" in Chapter 1. Chinese society develops in neither a linear nor a circular fashion. Instead, a spiral connotes a rolling, nonsequential form of development, in which contemporary society remains in some sense continuous with the past even as it looks to the future.

The most fully developed articulation of this pattern of development was given by Hegel, who saw himself as translating reflections on the nature of God into a comprehensive system organized around the intellectual intuition of the Whole. Hegel's concept of the Whole can be grasped through the notion of dialectics. For Hegel, dialectic is a movement that leads from an initial position through an opposing position to a new, third position that includes both the initial position and its opposite. "The world works in a spiral dynamic," Hegel writes. "The Whole is an overcoming which preserves what it overcomes" (1996, p.14). The Whole overcomes entities and ideas while simultaneously preserving them. Nothing is lost in this dynamic movement; residual formations are renewed and sustained at a higher level. This process takes the form of a spiral. For simplicity, it can be reduced to three steps: the "in-itself" (thesis), "out-of-itself" (antithesis), which stands in opposition to the thesis, and "in-and-for-itself," which is the solution or reconciliation. This last step, the synthesis, then becomes a new thesis, which is contradicted by a new antithesis that again pushes the dialectical triad to a higher level. Although this three-step process sounds repetitive, it actually gives rise to a progressive, spiral development because each synthesis adds something new. To compare the spiral dynamic with the alternation between day and night, "each day is different because of the experience of the previous night, and each night is different because of the experience of the preceding day" (Sameroff, 2010, p.10).

Hegel deals with ideal categories, not the real course of history. Several challenges must be overcome in applying Hegelian dialectics to history. To begin with, for Hegel, the dialectical movement of the Whole culminates in the human mind. How should I justify using Hegel's dialectics to examine social realities? On this point, I give a chronological account of the modernization path in China, treating social and conceptual history in parallel. I elaborate on how dialectical principles from the traditional Chinese belief system, Hegel and Marx, respectively, served the political needs of China's different modernization stages. I mean to discern a pattern that explains key policy changes in Chinese society. To achieve this, I have not adhered to a single theoretical paradigm but drawn freely from a range of interdisciplinary ideas about spiral: philosophy, politics, and cultural history. In so doing, I try to indicate how they cohere.

Another challenge concerns the universality of my theory. I do not intend to provide an all-inclusive, planet-wide history of ideas. Instead, I mean to grasp how China has developed in the context of the dominant, progressive worldview of modernity. In so doing, I have tried to find an alternative to the linear model of modernity—one that is better able to theorize social change, "modern" identities, technological "progress," and the relationship between ordinary people and knowledge authorities in China. The spiral society model, I claim, applies to China during its modernization. In laying out the framework of the spiral society, specific contexts are crucially important. Future researchers may want to test whether this framework applies to other countries. Indeed, it is well worth examining how countries with rich histories and longstanding traditions have remolded their cultural systems during the process of modernization and responded to its drawbacks.

I am also not concerned with predicting how history will develop or end. Consider Karl Marx's well-known inversion of Hegel:

> My dialectic method is not only different from the Hegelian, but is its direct opposite. To Hegel, the life process of the human brain, i.e., the process of thinking, which, under the name of "the Idea," he even transforms into an independent subject, is the *demiurgos* of the real world, and the real world is only the external, phenomenal form of "the Idea." With me, on the contrary, the ideal is nothing else than the material world reflected by the human mind, and translated into forms of thought (1971, p.29).

In Marx's thought, dialectics occur not just in the realm of the ideal, the human mind, but everywhere, every day. By arguing that history develops through dialectical contradictions, Marx (1971) transforms Hegel's idealistic dialectics into materialist, historical dialectics. For Marx, history develops in a spiral: an initial social formation is negated; that negation is then negated. In and through this process, characteristics of the original and subsequent social formations recur and are negated. He applies capitalism to this spiral model. According to him, in the first stage, capitalism negates communal ownership. In the second stage, as capitalism reaches its apogee in the forging of a world market, political crises occur, and class struggles lead to the overthrow of the bourgeoisie. In the third stage, although the mode of production will remain after the revolution, private property will be communally owned in the resulting social order. What is more, this will dissolve classes. Marx predicted that the global triumph of capitalism would mark the beginning of its dissolution. Nevertheless, as Gareth Stedman Jones has argued, their vision of "a spiral encircling the world with increasing speed and intensity and resulting in organic self-destruction came to nothing because the global economic crisis in 1857 did not lead to the return of revolution" (2019, p.229). To avoid theoretical difficulties in predicting the course of history, I do not plan to present a grand narrative about the movement of history. Instead, I only apply the spiral society model to China's period of modernization.

The dialectical tradition in China goes back to traditional philosophy. China's three major belief systems—Confucianism, Daoism, and Buddhism—are dialectical. For example, the Daoism diagram of darkness (*yin*) and brightness (*yang*) emphasizes that opposites are intertwined, as portrayed by the dark spot within the brightness and the bright spot within the darkness. According to Daoism, *yin* and *yang* are present in all things, and the motion of nature is something's movement towards its opposite. Dialectics can be found in Buddhism, one example being the mindset of the Prajna Paramita, according to which "emptiness is form, while form is emptiness" (*kong ji shi se, se ji shi kong*) (quoted in Ma, 2006, p. 59). Confucianism also has dialectical elements. The Confucian understanding of tradition, for example, is never static. Tradition has been translated as "*chuan tong*" in Chinese. Rendered literally, the character "*chuan*" means to continue, while the character "*tong*" means the essence of Confucianism. In short, tradition means important aspects of culture that have been passed down over generations.

Unlike Hegelian dialectics, however, traditional Chinese reasoning presents a dual structure rather than a triad process. It suggests analogical relations and complimentary pairs, such as *yin* and *yang*, *chuan* and *tong*, and thesis and antithesis. Influenced by the dual structure of dialectics in traditional philosophy, as I mentioned earlier, ancient Chinese people understood the dynastic change from the Qin Era right through to the Qing Era in terms of historical-dynastic cycles (*chao dai xun huan*).

Faced with the threat of Western invasions at the beginning of the twentieth century, reformers found ways of modernizing China. The 1911 Revolution overturned the Qing dynasty and established the Republic of China. Nevertheless, very few Chinese people felt that this represented a new beginning. Instead, they thought another dynasty cycle had begun. According to the historian Peter Zarrow,

> Even when the notion of revolution was understood as the overthrow of an entire political system, the term had originally simply referred to replacing the mandate of one dynasty with that of another, and it undoubtedly still carried the flavor of the dynastic cycle. (2006, p.10)

Zarrow found after the revolution, people expected a new dynasty rather than an entirely new political system following the fall of the Qing Dynasty. In *Monarchy of Republican China* (*gong he zhong de di zhi*), the historian Ming Zhang vividly described how ordinary people welcomed General Zhang Xun's efforts to restore the monarchy (2014), meaning they did not expect the monarchy system to be changed. In July 1917, Zhang Xun entered Beijing to reinstate the emperor of the Qing Dynasty. Before Zhang arrived in Beijing, people in Beijing hung dragon flags from their houses to welcome him, for the dragon symbolized monarchy in ancient society. Some of them had to use paper flags because those made out of fabric were sold out. Though the Qing

Dynasty was already replaced by the Republic of China, how people welcomed Xun Zhang indicates that people did not view the Republic of China as a breakaway from the previous dynasties.

Reformers tried to build a modern nation-state that would not fall back into another dynasty cycle while maintaining Chinese cultural integrity. A Chinese philosopher named Yuanpei Cai, who was famous for introducing Western thinking and synthesizing it with Chinese culture (Tian, 2005), systematically rethought Hegel's dialectics so that it applied to China's ambitions for modernization. For Cai, Hegelian dialectics legitimized the modernization of Chinese society:

> [Hegel's] dialectic is one that enlightens us in terms of a general view of things as evolution (growing, changing, and transforming). For him, things grow, change, and transform through complementarity in opposition; there is no other way by which things can evolve from the inorganic world into the plant, animal, or even human. (1984, p.196)

In Yuanpei Cai's interpretation of Hegel, first, Hegel's dialectics indicate that traditional Chinese society can transform itself into a Euro-American form of modernity, for Chinese tradition and Western modernity are opposite yet complementary. Second, compared with the dual structure in traditional Chinese dialectics, Hegel's dialectics is evolutionary. It focuses on achieving social development by way of contradictions. Although Yuanpei Cai did not postulate a three-step Hegelian process in this paragraph, he implied that traditional Chinese society could be transformed into a more advanced society by incorporating Western technology, political institutions, and ideologies that contradicted its own traditions.

The changes wrought by China's modernization can be understood through the lens of Hegel's three-part process, adapted to fit Chinese contexts: *modernization*, *reversals*, and *new forms of modernization*. This spiral progression begins with the initial modernization of the existing social structure. It then proceeds with reversals, where policymakers and authorities address the limitations of modernization by partially reversing certain aspects of the process. However, these reversals are not complete; instead, they retain some elements of the original social structure.

My conception of spiral development acknowledges that it may backtrack to some degree. Modernization does not irrevocably alter society, separating us forever from our primitive, pre-modern ancestors. Chinese society evolved in a spiral fashion in response to the challenges posed by modernization. This does not imply that these responses are always successful but rather that they reflect the dynamic nature of Chinese society, driven by its inherent contradictions.

Furthermore, spiral modernization suggests that society does not simply regress; rather, it gives rise to new social formations that incorporate both reversals and elements of the original structure. For instance, the tension between tradition and modernization exemplifies one such contradiction. It is not uncommon for Chinese political leaders to draw inspiration from tradition amidst the modernization process. Tradition acts as a cohesive force within society, offering solutions to modernization-related issues. Thus, the concept of spiral modernization breaks down dualities—namely those between tradition and modernity, tradition and westernization, construction and deconstruction, linearity and circularity. It highlights the complex interplay between these elements.

Four spirals

Now, I will delineate the spiral modernization path of Chinese society across four historical periods: the transition from the late Qing Dynasty to the Republican Era, the Mao Era, the Deng Era, and the Xi Era. The trajectory of Chinese modernization between the late Qing Dynasty and the Republican Era constitutes a spiral change in societal norms and values within Chinese society. During this period, reformers endeavored to assimilate lessons from the modernized West. China's New Culture Movement, for example, saw universities incorporating Western philosophy into their academic programs while activists advocated for the adoption of Western political ideologies such as democracy, republicanism, and liberalism.

However, embracing Westernization led to concerns about corruption and moral decadence. Westernization was linked with "hedonism, laziness, and unbearable filthiness" (Dirlik, 1975, p.954). Intellectuals observed a rise in behaviors like smoking, gambling, and pursuit of pleasure. They believed these behaviors undermined social cohesion and moral integrity.

Despite these challenges, reformers remained committed to the pursuit of Western modernization. To underscore the importance of morality in the modernization process, they turned to Confucianism for inspiration, even though Confucianism was dismissed in the New Culture Movement. Confucianism was lauded for its emphasis on virtues and ethics, such as diligence and filial piety (Qin, 1953). The proponents of the New Life Movement, spearheaded by Republican President Jieshi Jiang and his wife, Meiling Song, advocated for the revival of Confucian values as a remedy for the moral and political dilemmas posed by Westernization (Jiang, 1934). Lin He, the head teacher of the Central Political School of Kuomingtang (*guo ming dang zhong yang zheng zhi xue xiao*), provided intellectual legitimacy to President Jiang's New Life Movement through his dialectical interpretation of Confucianism. Utilizing Hegel's dialectics, he claimed that "modern thought and culture should not be separated from the past" (1917, p.1). According to him, Confucianism and Westernization are complementary, and Confucianism could enrich Western culture.

However, the repackaging of Confucianism within the New Life Movement did not signify a regression to the norms of the Qing Dynasty era. Instead, it presented Confucian ethics within the framework of modernization. As Paul Linebarger, an American scholar living in China during the Republic era, wrote, "it is [the New Life Movement's] principles consist of a simple restatement of the cardinal Confucian personal virtues, interpreted to suit modern conditions" (1938, p.61).

Throughout the Republican Era, China suffered from economic decline, unequal treaties with Western powers, and Japan's invasion. As a result, some Chinese reformers came to the realization that neither Westernization nor Confucianism alone could revitalize the nation. The aftermath of the 1917 Russian Revolution saw a growing attraction to Marxism among Chinese intellectuals, marking the onset of another phase in China's spiral of modernization. In this phase, policy reversals were initiated by a localized adaptation of Marxist dialectics within China.

Before I describe this spiral, it is essential to understand how Marxism was adapted to the Chinese context. As the Asian studies scholar Arif Dirlik (1997) has remarked, "the Marxism (Marxism-Leninism) that Chinese Communists inherited was a Marxism that had already been 'deterritorialized' from its original terrain in European history and was reterritorialized upon a Chinese terrain" (p.613-14). China's nascent capitalist economy posed challenges for applying traditional Marxist principles. To cross this "Caudine Folks" (Marx 1872, p.353), Chairman Mao reinterpreted Marx's materialist/historical dialectics. Drawing from Hegel's dialectics in Logic, Marx's approach viewed contradictions as drivers of social change. Mao further radicalized this notion by emphasizing the perpetual "struggle between opposites."[5] According to Mao,

> Such unity...... as we see in daily life, are all appearances of things in the state of quantitative change. On the other hand, the dissolution of unity...... the change of each into its opposite are all appearances of things in a state of qualitative change, the transformation of one process into another. That is why we say that the unity of opposites is

---

[5] In 321 B.C. the Samnites defeated the Roman army near the Caudine Pass and forced them to cross the Forks. Caudine Forks refers to great challenges that a country faces during the development. Marx thought Russia might cross the Caudine Forks. Russia might achieve socialism without experiencing capitalism.

conditional, temporary, and relative, while the struggle of mutually
exclusive opposites is absolute (1937, p.498, translation modified)

In Mao's view, Chinese society was rife with contradictions between various
factions: tradition versus modernity, the proletariat versus the bourgeoisie, and
Eastern nations versus Western imperialism. Mao believed that through
continuous struggles, the oppressed classes would eventually triumph, leading
to the establishment of socialism in China. This framework justified Mao's
emphasis on class struggles and the need for perpetual revolution, bypassing
the capitalist stage of development (Zhang, 2004).

To promote the "struggle of opposites," Chairman Mao launched several
campaigns against the policies of the Republic Era. Both Western and
traditional Chinese cultures were attacked. For instance, during the Cultural
Revolution, people who had ties with the former Nationalist government were
labeled class enemies and persecuted. Intellectuals who promoted the Western
model of modernization or studied abroad were branded petty bourgeois.
During the movement's heyday, they were sent to remote areas for re-education
of socialism. As part of the destruction of the Four Olds (*po si jiu*) during the
Maoist Era, traditional Chinese culture was harshly criticized. Confucianism
was treated as an obstacle in the path of the revolution. The Red Guards (*hong
wei bing*) even destroyed the Temple of Confucius in Shandong Province.
Through these policy reversals, Chairman Mao believed the Proletariat would
gain power one day, and China would eventually reach socialism.

However, the policy reversals under Chairman Mao did not signify a complete
rejection of Western or traditional Chinese influences on society. Despite his
anti-Western rhetoric, Mao maintained careful negotiations in China's
international relationships. He aligned closely with Third World countries in
Africa and Latin America while also seeking to ease tensions with Europe.
China's entry into the United Nations in 1971 and the historic visit by US
President Richard Nixon in 1972 marked a divergence between its diplomatic
strategies and domestic policies.

Since Mao's era, materialist dialectics have been enshrined in the
Communist Party's constitution. "For party leaders, adhering to materialist
dialectics improves their abilities to solve the problems of China's reform and
development" (Xinhua, 2015). The transition from Mao's rule to Deng's
premiership constitutes another spiral in China's modernization trajectory.
Mao's policies, notably the Cultural Revolution, resulted in humanitarian crises
and social upheavals. "Millions of people suffered public humiliation,
imprisonment, torture, hard labor, the seizure of their property, and sometimes
death...... Estimates of the Cultural Revolution's death toll vary greatly, ranging
from hundreds of thousands to 20 million" (Pye, 1986, p.598). The closure of

schools and the purge of intellectuals sharply curbed technological development. Economic activity came to a halt during the Cultural Revolution. To address these challenges, Deng initiated policy reversals. His approach, encapsulated in the phrase "No debate" (quoted in Chen, 1999, p.450), signaled a departure from Mao's ideological struggles toward a pragmatic, results-oriented strategy. The phrase "No debate" indicates that whether a development strategy is Western or Chinese, capitalist or socialist, no longer matters. He did not cast socialism in opposition to capitalism. He launched market-economy reforms. He also welcomed Western technology.

However, Deng did not call for total Westernization and privatization. For example, despite adopting market-oriented measures to stimulate growth and productivity, Deng ensured that the government retained control over critical sectors such as land. As he said during the opening ceremony of the Twelfth Party's Congress, "both revolution and construction require learning from foreign experience. However, copying the experiences and models of other countries has never been successful" (quoted in People, 2016). His phrase "Modernization with Chinese Characteristics" (*zhong guo te se de xian dai hua*) (quoted in People, 2016) indicates a new form of modernization that combines both characteristics of the Mao Era and the revision of Mao's policies. As Chairman Jiang (2000) summarized,[6]

> He did not get rid of Marxism-Leninism and Chairman Mao Zedong's thoughts. Losing Marxism-Leninism and Chairman Mao Zedong's thoughts would shake the foundation of our country. At the same time, he focused on the actual problems of the country's modernization......He applied Marxist theories to fit new development.

Deng recognized the importance of preserving Marxism-Leninism and Mao Zedong's thoughts as foundational to the Communist Party's ideology.

The contemporary Chinese society is in another spiral. As exemplified by the tensions between ARTs as power technologies and uncertainty of ARTs, Chairman Deng's modernization strategies have brought national development but also resulted in unintended side effects. Side effects involved worship of technology, declining fertility rates, and social conflicts. "In this scenario, what [political leaders] will be forced to consider is how to assess and even retreat from certain reforming programs that are endangering the future

---

[6] Chairman Zemin Jiang succeeded Chairman Xiaoping Deng. He acted as general secretary of the Chinese Communist Party (CCP) from 1989 to 2002, as chairman of the Central Military Commission from 1989 to 2004, and as president of China from 1993 to 2003.

of China" (Tian, 2019, p.35). Political leaders reversed Chairman Deng's policies to address side effects. Both returning to tradition and tightening political control are antithetical to what Chairman Deng had recommended. Nowadays, Chinese political leaders preserve and promote traditional values. For instance, Chairman Hu adopted the traditional philosophy of harmony in response to social conflicts wrought by modernization. Despite tradition often being seen as at odds with modernization, it serves as a stabilizing force in contemporary society. Chairman Xi has initiated crackdowns on civil societies and emphasized his own personal charisma, echoing Chairman Mao's approach to reinforce control. This tightening of political control contradicts Deng's narratives of a more open society, aiming instead to maintain social stability.

Yet, these leaders have not entirely abandoned Chairman Deng's policies. Repackaging tradition does not signify a complete reversal of historical progress. Science and technology remain central to China's political agenda, as emphasized by Chairman Xi at the 20th Academician Congress of the Chinese Academy of Sciences in 2021 (Government of People's Republic of China, 2022). Likewise, while strengthening political control, the party leaders have not reverted to the Mao era's rapid centralization of the economy. China's current development path combines economic and social openness with a firm political grip, reflecting a spiral development where modernization and its reversals coalesce into a new form of modernization — the New Era.

Summary

This chapter provided the historical background of China's modernization policies from the 1980s and introduced a concept called spiral modernization to explain the twists and turns along the path of Chinese modernization. I first elaborated on the challenges posed by Chairman Deng's policies on technology development, Late Marriage and Late Childbearing, social open-up, free market, and political restructuring. As demonstrated, technology development can easily lead to its abuse, while Late Marriage and Late Childbearing result in fertility decline. Social open-up results in sexual liberalization and Westernization, the free market privatizes the medical system, and political restructuring fosters conflicts between ordinary people and officials. I then introduced how Chairman Xi's government addresses these challenges by promoting two policy reversals: repackaging traditional Chinese culture and tightening political control. Finally, drawing from Hegel's dialectics, I presented the concept of spiral modernization and elaborated on the four stages of spiral development during the Chinese modernization path from the Late Qing dynasty to Chairman Xi's New Era.

Foregrounding the historical background in this chapter is essential because it helps understand how ARTs regulations are intertwined with social, political, and cultural contexts in China. Building on the analysis provided in this chapter, the subsequent chapter will analyze an instance of spiral modernization by examining how the uncertainty of ARTs informs over-reliance on technology. It will also explore how clinicians brought up a traditional idea called *Ming* to prevent technology misuse.

Chapter 3

Uncertain outcomes

Life and death are predestined: wealth and honor reside in heaven (sheng si you Ming, fu gui zai tian).
—Confucius, *Analects of Confucius*

Ming

One day, I encountered a man who distributed leaflets for "magic tablets" outside P Clinic. According to his leaflet, the magic tablets could rapidly cure orthopedic diseases, claiming patients could walk by themselves just one day after taking the medicine. The purported magic power of these tablets reminded me of the couple who protested outside P Clinic. They claimed the clinic should take full responsibility for their child's cerebra palsy. Their claim was based on the assumption that omnipotent biotechnological solutions could cure any disease. Nevertheless, research findings confirm the difficulty in ruling out fetal deformity before childbirth (Davies et al., 2012; Boulet et al., 2016; Liberman et al., 2017; Mussa et al., 2017; Luke et al., 2021).

The couple's experience made me assume that ARTs are limited in medical conditions due to low success rates. By success, I refer to the birth of healthy babies. There are various measures of ARTs success, including embryo fertilization rates, pregnancy rates, singleton live birth rates, and multiple live birth rates. Some clinics tend to market only embryo fertilization rates or pregnancy rates to show high success rates of their treatment. However, not all implantation cycles lead to pregnancy, and pregnancy does not necessarily mean live birth. Even if children are born successfully, there might still be risks of adverse outcomes for mothers and children, such as cesarean section, prematurity, low birth weight, and infant disability. According to a nationwide survey of 445 clinics located in 31 provinces of mainland China in 2018 (98.7% of the licensed fertility clinics in China were covered in this survey) (Bai et al., 2020) between 1st January to 31st December 2016 there were 906840 IVF cycles performed in mainland China. The clinical pregnancy rate per egg retrieval cycle was 23.2%, while the delivery rate per egg retrieval cycle decreased to 18.7%. The total number of live infants born in mainland China in 2016 was 18.46 million, but the number of infants born through ATRs was only 311,309, which accounted for 1.69% of the total. The reported rate of birth defects among infants born through ARTs was rare, but it still accounted for about 0.87%.[1]

To my surprise, however, low success rates were not the primary consideration behind the regulations. For clinicians, although they are low, the overall success rates of ARTs can still be predicted. Consider an article shared on the WeChat platform, which claims that P Clinic raises public awareness of infertility treatment. The article, titled "Introduction of IVF in P Clinic" (source anonymized, 2013), indicates clinicians can predict IVF success rates according to factors such as patient's age, ovarian function, and hormone levels. For the clinicians addressed during my fieldwork, such as IVF success rates, egg freezing success rates were also calculable. Dr. L (2016a), a fertility specialist at P Clinic, made this clear:

> Clinicians will determine the dosage of ovulation drugs according to patients' basal FSH. Overdosage leads to ovarian hyper-stimulation. Patients will take anesthesia before egg retrieval... The success rate depends on age. The overall success rate is 50%.

Another fertility specialist, J Hospital's Dr. W (2016), explained this in more depth:

> The risks of egg freezing nowadays are not high. In previous years, ice crystallization damage was a potential risk. However, vitrification enables successful egg freezing without ice crystallization. The risks of egg freezing are as low as those of IVF. The success rate is related to egg quality and endometrial thickness. The success rate for young eggs can exceed 70%.

Both clinicians said they could predict whether a patient would be successful in freezing egg rates according to their age, the quality of the sperm they are using, and endometrial thickness.

What clinicians were really concerned about was individual cases, such as whether ARTs can lead to healthy live births, which is often inconsistent with clinical or scientific prediction. Indeed, during my visit to P Clinic, I found that pregnancy results sometimes do not match clinicians' expectations. Yuanhong, who was 40 years of age, received IVF treatment at P Clinic. Her first cycle had failed; this was her second attempt. I was talking to her in the waiting lounge, next to a "results machine," while she was waiting for her test results. She burst

---

[1] In comparison the birth defects rate of natural pregnancies was 2.3% (Wei et al, 2023).

into tears as soon as she found out that she was pregnant. She (2016) did not believe in the results, saying:

> I feel excited. At the same time, I am worried. I tried IVF before. The implantation was also successful. I told my mother-in-law the good news. My mother-in-law was so happy that she told almost everyone in my village. When I returned to the village, my relatives even set up fireworks to celebrate my pregnancy. However, after two months, the fetus stopped growing. I could not feel the pain during curettage surgery because my heart was broken … no matter how advanced the technology is, every technology can lead to both success and failure.

Although Yuanhong's first embryo implantation was successful, and hence clinicians were confident in her treatment, she did not conceive a child. Through this experience, she realized that clinicians' predictions did not necessarily lead to satisfactory results for individual users of IVF.

Chanjuan, a 30-year-old woman pursuing IVF treatment at P Clinic, had a comparable experience. Given her age, in theory, she had a high chance of becoming pregnant. Her doctor was confident that her treatment would be successful. Indeed, age is one of the main indicators of successful fertility treatment. For example, according to UK Statistics for IVF and DI Treatment, Storage and Donation published by the Human Fertilisation and Embryology Authority (HFEA) in 2020, in 2019, the birth rates of IVF treatment for patients who were under 35 years old were 32% per embryo transferred, while the birth rates for patients who were over 43 years old were only 5%. Nevertheless, Chanjuan failed three times. Looking back at the experience of her treatment, she realized the unforeseen results of her fertility treatment.

The clinicians accounted for discrepancies between scientific and statistical predictions on the one hand and individual cases on the other by referring to *Ming. Ming* is a fundamental element of the traditional Chinese belief system. The earliest writings in which *Ming* appears are oracle bone inscriptions from the Shang Dynasty. Some inscriptions associate *Ming* with an almighty force, *Di*, which determined the unfolding of all things. When people living during the Shang Dynasty encountered uncertainty (regarding when rain would come, for instance, or when the harvest should be brought in), they sought out signs by reading the cracks in bones. In this way, they hoped to divine *Di*'s will. In these contexts, *Ming* could be interpreted as a heavenly mandate determining human life. *Ming* indicates the ways in which human beings are inherently linked to heaven. As such, it was the given status of personal destiny. The idea of "*Ming*" is then manifested in a variety of Chinese sayings, such as "if it is one's fate to die in a well, then drowning in a river will not be fatal" (*Ming gai jin li si, he li yan bu sha*); "if one's fate is eight inches, it is difficult to attain a foot" (*Ming li ba chi, nan qiu yi zhang*); and "if one's fate is to be unsuccessful, one should accept poverty, for wealth and honor are forged in heaven" (*Ming li wu cai gai shou qiong, fu gui dou shi tian zhu cheng*). Those popular sayings or proverbs imply that one's *Ming* is what it is.

I was conscious that my interviewees described ARTs in terms such as "uncertain," "unknown," and "uncontrollable" rather than explicitly confirming the risks or disadvantages of the technologies. It is important to distinguish this uncertainty from concepts such as "dispositional optimism" (Devroe et al., 2022, p. 997) and "false hope" (Mohapatra, 2013, p.392; Jacob and Balen 2018, p. 200) invested in fertility treatment. Although these terms also indicate the unreliability of ARTs, they refer to calculated success rates based on factors such as patients' age and test results. The uncertainty highlighted in this chapter, by contrast, stems from the inherent unpredictability of patients' destinies. Hence, the uncertainty discussed here is metaphysical, not statistical.

According to the traditional doctrines of *Ming*, if a woman is destined to have children, she will get pregnant even if she steers clear of fertility treatment. Indeed, the apparent miracle of "getting pregnant coincidentally" (to use the words of one interviewee) often revealed a lot about patients seeking fertility treatment at P Clinic. Here, I present two stories from the fieldwork, suggesting how technological interventions can become meaningless in the face of *Ming*. Yuetong underwent infertility treatment in the P clinic and eventually became pregnant. She was so excited that she engaged in an interview with me along with another patient. She (2016) described the surprise of finding out that she was pregnant in the following way:

> In the first month, I relied on an artificial cycle. Strangely, there were no egg follicles or cell membranes. I was very disappointed. In the second month, I relied on an artificial cycle again. There were still no egg follicles and cell membranes. I felt so anxious that I drank a bottle of beer. I never drank any alcohol before because it was harmful to the fetus. In the third month, I tried a natural cycle. You know what? Cell membranes grew well. Was it weird? Later, I began to drink beer once a week or when I hung out with my friends. I got pregnant.

Ruyi (2016), who conducted two cycles of IVF treatment in the clinic, also experienced the miracle of pregnancy after drinking alcohol:

> During my first cycle, I gave up drinking. Well, I did not give up drinking completely. I did not drink too much. Is one bottle of beer or two glasses

of wine too much for girls? Even though I gave up drinking, I failed to get pregnant. I was so upset that I drank a glass of whiskey. I never drank whiskey before. Can you guess the result? I got pregnant after my second cycle. To conceive children, people should follow *Ming*. If you have children in *Ming*, then you will have children.

  Both Yuetong and Ruyi were struggling to understand their mysterious reproductive journeys. Fearing that alcohol might harm their fetuses, they initially quit drinking in order to get pregnant. Indeed, existing studies show that alcohol is known for its detrimental effect on female fecundability (Fan et al., 2017). Yuetong and Ruyi's teetotalism, however, did not help. On the contrary, they got pregnant after they started drinking again. Given that no medical evidence could explain why they got pregnant after drinking alcohol, they invoked *Ming* to make the connection. Their becoming pregnant after drinking, they supposed, was not a random miracle; it was destined to occur. The themes of surprise and luck are prominent in many studies on fertility treatment. For example, Jordanna Isaacson (2018) discovered when women were able to retrieve a greater number of high-quality eggs than expected, they perceived themselves as fortunate and felt more optimistic about their chances of conceiving. However, in Jordanna's study, luck connotes randomness. Yuetong and Ruyi, in contrast, saw their reproductive fortunes as predestined.

  Advanced technologies cannot alter patients' *Ming*. If a woman does not have children in *Ming*, no matter how many cycles of ARTs she pursues, she will not have children. Speaking of a patient who had tried IVF a few times, Dr. L (2016b) remarked that "if she is destined to have children, then she will have children. If not, no matter how many times she tries, she will fail. Patients rely too much on technology. What we can do is limited in the face of human destiny." According to Dr. L, the patient's failures of fertility treatment indicate that she might not have children in *Ming*. Dr. L implied the patient should not over-rely on IVF.

  Clinicians who are supposed to believe in their scientific expertise also cannot change or even anticipate patients' *Ming*. They do not know if fertility treatment will or will not work in advance. No matter how smoothly a given fertility treatment goes, clinicians will only know the result first after they find out whether the woman is pregnant and then when the woman's children are born. Meiyu visited P Clinic to implant two frozen embryos. At first, the embryos grew well. The embryos were bigger than normal, leading Dr. D to predict that she would conceive twins. Nevertheless, the embryos stopped growing after eight weeks. Meiyu could not believe this and insisted on having an additional Ultra-B wave test to confirm it. Dr. D (2016a) comforted her by saying, "It is unnecessary to take another test. I know you are disappointed, but no one could predict the result. We can only wait until children are born." Meiyu's story indicates that optimism based on modern science and technology is often misplaced. In addition, Dr. D's statement that "we can only wait until children are born" reflects her feeling of powerlessness in the face of *Ming*. She asked Meiyu to wait, but she had no definite answers when pressed on how long she would have to wait. *Ming*, it would seem, is revealed only at the right time. People cannot anticipate when that time is; they can only await its arrival.

Dr. D's interpretation of the timing of reproduction closely resembles stories contained in Liu Xiang's *Categorized Biographies of Women* (*Lie Nv Zhuan*) from 18 BCE, the earliest book aimed at educating women in China. One biography relates to the wife of Ling of Zhao. Well-known for her morality and virtue, she was infertile for many years. One day, she dreamt of a woman who sang of a beautiful girl as yet unborn. "Oh *Ming*, Oh *Ming*," she sang, "when she meets the time of Heaven, she will be born" (Liu 1983, p.42). Heaven controls individual destinies; it was to endow Ling of Zhao's wife with a child when the right time came. Before that moment, however, she could only wait.

The obscure temporality of *Ming* served to explain the asynchronies in patients' reproductive journeys. By asynchronies, I mean the way in which some women's treatments failed several times before they finally conceived children successfully. One day, at the end of Dr. D's consultation session, a woman came in to present her with red eggs and candies. In China, the families of newborn babies send red eggs and candies as gifts to friends and relatives. Dr. D (2016b) was surprised to hear of the woman's pregnancy:

> How interesting this case is. For several years, she was infertile for no reason. She tried IVF several times but failed. And since she did not freeze extra embryos, she had to give up IVF. Surprisingly, after she returned home, she found that she was pregnant. She got pregnant naturally. This is *Ming*. You can write about this case in your research. This lady conducted a laparoscopy, which did not discover her disease. She tried IVF but failed. Then she gave up and returned home. You know what? She got pregnant. Her *Ming* is so good. If you have children in your *Ming*, you will finally have children.

Dr. D attributed the woman's pregnancy to *Ming* because she could not identify the reasons for either her initial infertility or sudden natural pregnancy. The woman, she explained, was destined to have children. But if the woman had children in her *Ming*, why did her IVF treatments fail on several occasions? The woman had not conceived at first, Dr. D claimed, because she had not yet reached the time at which it was predestined that she would get pregnant.

Although *Ming* had marked her as a mother, it took some time for this to be realized. When the right moment arrived, she got pregnant even without the help of ARTs.

After all, clinicians with advanced knowledge about reproductive technologies cannot tell patients when the right time set by *Ming* might arrive. They comforted patients by asking them to wait. However, so-called fortunetellers claim that they know whether people would have children in *Ming*. Rongfang was 35 and had just succeeded in her first IVF cycle before our interview. She was not surprised at her pregnancy because a fortuneteller told her that she had both a boy and a girl in her *Ming*. "I was married for five years and did not have children," Rongfang (2016) told me:

> I went to several hospitals, but doctors told us that we did not have any diseases. We decided not to have any treatment. If we have children in *Ming*, we will have children eventually. If we do not have children in *Ming*, I can adopt a child … Conceiving children is not like buying groceries at the supermarket. In a supermarket, you can buy whatever you want. … I almost gave up until I met a fortuneteller. I asked him when I would have children. The fortuneteller said that I would have a child this year. I then asked him why I had not had children for so many years. He said I had not reached the time to have children. He said I would be sure to have a child this year.

Rongfang used the metaphor of the supermarket as a contrast class to imply that people have few options when trying to conceive children. *Ming*, rather than people, determines childbirth. Hence, her narrative emphasized the importance of waiting and patience. What is significant in her story is she openly admitted the importance of fortunetelling in her reproductive journey. It was the fortuneteller, as opposed to clinicians and modern technology, that assured her that she was destined to have a boy and a girl. The fortuneteller even knew when she would have children.

Rongfang's narrative about fortunetelling reminded me of my own experience with a palm reader outside the P clinic. One day, a lady stopped me and asked if I wanted to know the fate of my marriage or when I would have children. As I did not plan to talk to her, I replied without thinking. "I do not plan to have children now," I told her. I thought that she would turn to other people who were pursuing fertility treatment. Perhaps she misunderstood my meaning. Surprisingly, she became very excited to hear my answer and proceeded to follow me, "You're wrong. It is not that you are not meant to have children. It is that your children have not yet come" (Palm Reader, 2016). The palm reader's comments implied that although *Ming* dictated that I would have children, the time for my pregnancy had not come. She (2016) claimed that she was able to facilitate the timing of *Ming*:

> Your children will come immediately when you use my methods. You should hang a landscape painting in your bedroom corner. Children love landscape paintings. Do not hang animal photos such as *pi xiu* (a mythical wild animal in Chinese folk tales) and tigers, which will frighten babies away. There must be enough sunshine in the bedroom because sunshine can reconcile yin and yang and make women pregnant. Do not put a bathtub or a mirror in your bedroom. Bathtubs and mirrors will not only frighten away babies and consume men's sperm.

This palm reader did not attempt to alter my *Ming*. Instead, she imbued ordinary actions, such as hanging landscape paintings, with extraordinary significance. These actions became rituals that bridged the divide between people and heavenly *Ming* and facilitated a reduction in waiting times. Therefore, I do not perceive her role as contradicting the argument that people are powerless in the face of *Ming*. Her prominent role lies in her claim to understand the mysteries of heavenly destiny and in developing methods to help me cope with the waiting process, while clinicians armed with scientific knowledge simply asked patients to wait. In this sense, the omnipotence of modern technologies is further undermined.

The following nature

In the previous section, I demonstrated treatment outcomes of ARTs are uncertain. *Ming*, rather than ARTs or doctors, determines treatment outcomes. It is surprising that this traditional idea of *Ming* pervaded my interviewees' narratives. The uncertainty brought by *Ming* recalls a fundamental human experience that has faded with the development of modern societies across the world. In ancient societies, humanity was preoccupied with uncertainty—the state of not knowing (and therefore being unable to control) the future and state of the world. With limited knowledge about the world, people attributed unexpected encounters and unavoidable events to supernatural forces, such as premature death, starvation, epidemics, and natural disasters. *Ming* served as one of these supernatural forces in ancient China, while in ancient Greece, Moirai (fate) played a similar role.

However, from the twelfth and thirteenth centuries in Europe, supernatural forces gradually lost their authority in various aspects of life. The following passage, from the historian of the Italian Renaissance Jacob Burckhardt, is instructive in this regard:

> In the Middle Ages both sides of human consciousness ... lay dreaming or half awake beneath a common veil. The veil was woven of faith, illusion, and childish prepossession, through which the world and history were seen clad in strange hues. ... It is in Italy that this veil first melted into the air: an objective treatment and consideration of the State and of all the things of this world became possible... Modern man became a spiritual individual, and recognized himself as such. (1954, p.131).

According to Burckhardt, the minds of modern individuals were no longer veiled by religious dogma. With the development of science and technology, reason became the primary source of legitimacy in social practice. According to Walter Benjamin, a philosopher on modernity, rationality—especially instrumental rationality—is a "hallmark of modernity" (quoted in Frisby, 1988, p.194). People began to act according to rational calculation and planning to contend with the future (Beckert, 2016).

As people began to understand the world through reason grounded in evidence, a new way to deal with uncertainty spread through Europe. People reduced the uncontrollable uncertainty to specific, calculable risks. As historian Peter Bernstein wrote in his book *Against the Gods*, "the revolutionary idea that defines the boundary between modern times and the past is the mastery of risk: the notion that the future is more than a whim of the gods and that men and women are not passive before nature" (1998, p.1). Risks are measured in terms of probabilities, through which the future is statistically predicted. One example is the insurance market developing in mid-sixteenth-century Europe. For merchants and seafarers with insurance, uncertain storms were reduced to the probability that one's vessel might be wrecked. The risks and success rates of ARTs are akin to these probabilities—they are quantifiable.

Similarly to their Western counterparts, Chinese attitudes toward uncertainty have evolved over time, with *Ming* and fortune-telling being increasingly labeled as "superstitious" (*mi xin*) or heterodox with the modernization of society. Many believe they can change destiny. During the Mao era, for example, state socialism heavily emphasized the idea that individuals shape their lives through individual agency, rather than divine order. According to Chairman Mao (2021), "If [people] take their destiny into their own hands......instead of evading them, there will be no difficulty in the world which they cannot overcome." However, in the Mao era, an individual's capacity was constrained by their class. As Mao (2021) argues, "In a class society, individuals live according to their class status, and their thoughts are determined by class......the responsibility of changing the world lies on the proletariat." On the contrary, under Chairman Deng's leadership, the slogan "everyone is the maker of his own destiny" (*mei ge ren dou neng wei zi ji de ming yun fen dou*) (Xinhua, 2018) encouraged people, regardless of class, to embrace risks. For example, many Chinese people smashed so-called "iron rice bowls" (*tie fan wan*) (BBC Online Network, 1999). Iron rice bowls are referred to as guaranteed job security. Prior to Chairman Deng's reforms, most employers were state-owned enterprises and institutions that ensured employees received the same salary regardless of their performance. After Chairman Deng's reforms, many Chinese people challenged lifelong job security, bravely venturing from villages to urban areas in search of work or engaging in trade with foreign companies. In his speech celebrating the 40-year anniversary of Chairman Deng's Open and Reform Policy, Chairman Xi (2018) remarked that "in the past 40 years, Chinese people, who are in control of their own destiny, have shown unprecedented enthusiasm, initiative, creativity, and power in the Open and Reform Policy and socialist modernization."

Against this backdrop, the uncertain outcomes of ARTs, as determined by the traditional belief in *Ming*, are reimagined in contemporary Chinese society. This implies that my interviewees had realized the limits of human efforts to control reproduction. Using modern technologies to change *Ming*, according to Dr. D's traditional view of the world, would not yield positive outcomes. She (2016c) shared the example of her friend, Dr. Y.

> Clinics in the US often brag about the magic power of their advanced technologies. My friend Dr. Y, who is also a clinician, insisted on going to the US for IVF treatment. I conducted tocolysis (*baotai*) for her. Her first child was a daughter. She wanted a boy for her second child. Thus, she went to the US to try IVF and perform sex selection.[2] After she returned to China and registered with our hospital, she found she had not become pregnant. Now she has got pregnant naturally, though she does not know the sex of the baby. She felt exhausted, having traveled to the US.

For Dr. D, as both pregnancy and biological sex were determined by *Ming*, people should not alter them. Her friend Dr. Y, who tried to intervene in her baby's sex, eventually failed. Likewise, one article shared on P Clinic's WeChat

---

[2] While sex selection during pregnancy is not uncommon in China, leading to a population sex imbalance skewed in favor of males, it's worth noting that sex selection, including through assisted reproductive technologies (ARTs) in private clinics, is illegal in the country. Despite this legal prohibition, some individuals still seek out these services in pursuit of having children of their preferred sex.

platform urged women not to put their hopes in freezing eggs to pause the biological clock:

> Do not freeze eggs to postpone pregnancy. Egg freezing should not be widely promoted. The government has already abolished welfare for late marriage and late childbearing. Although conceiving children requires that women balance work and family and have enough economic resources, women still need to follow nature and conceive children early. Social egg freezing does not necessarily lead to successful childbirth. Do not trust aphrodisiac advertisements or go to private clinics. Private clinics only ask for money (source anonymized, 2014).

The article acknowledges that women may have various personal motivations for delaying childbirth, yet it strongly advises against using technology for this purpose. It cautions that such technological interventions are unlikely to yield positive outcomes, asserting that social egg freezing is a waste of money.

My interviewees did not criticize ARTs directly, but instead, they employed the traditional idea of *Ming* to decry the excessive reliance on these technologies. Such reflection serves as the driving force behind the evolution of a spiral society. Indeed, the misuse of ARTs has led to social and environmental disasters. According to the introduction of the *Book*, since ARTs clinics have mushroomed across China since the 1990s, surrogacy schemes, unlicensed technologies (that were still in an experimental phase), and multiple births have been widely abused (Yu et al., 2015, p.12). The consequences of misusing technology, Dr. D pointed out, include (but are not limited to) retarded development among children and a burden on the social welfare system.

Similarly, the *Book* describes a 45-year-old Argentinean woman who conceived twins using her frozen eggs. This broke the world record for the longest duration between egg freezing and subsequent conception. The *Book* uses this example to illustrate that one can "never know if science will bring us joy or a shock" (Yu et al., 2015, p.48.) Although Monica conceived children successfully at 45, clinicians remain uncertain about whether the length of time for which eggs are frozen influences the health of the resulting children. Therefore, the *Book* advocates for placing limitations on ARTs.

My interviewees associated ARTs with other methods of defying, changing, and controlling *Ming*. According to Dr. D (2016c),

> We (clinicians) do not support plastic surgery. People should not cut their bones in order to grow taller. Another example of human

intervention is the urbanization of China. The government cuts down trees in order to build more cities. Now they realize the problems that have brought about and demolish buildings to plant more trees. China has learned a lot of lessons. European countries are good at following nature. Many reproduction technologies are restricted in European countries.[3] In sharp contrast, the U.S. is crazy for new developments in ARTs. People are able to conceive six babies at the same time with the help of ARTs. ARTs are completely commercialized in the U.S. We should follow nature.

Dr. D raised two interesting points. Firstly, she compared ARTs with urbanization, another outcome of Chairman Deng's modernization policies. Dr. D expressed significant concerns about the adverse effects of urbanization, which she deemed "anti-natural," condemning the government's practice of "[cutting] down trees in order to build more cities." Indeed, as I discussed in Chapter 2, Chinese urbanization has led to numerous environmental problems, such as air pollution and deforestation.

Secondly, Dr. D particularly disapproved of the American ways of using ARTs. She thought they were especially radicalized and commercialized. "The United States is crazy for new developments in ARTs," she told me. "People are able to conceive six babies at the same time with the help of ARTs. ..." (Dr. D, 2016c). She said that the clinics involved had failed to anticipate the serious consequences of multiple births. However, it's important to acknowledge that her findings represent a selective portrayal of American ART practices. Multiple births are not standard practice in the U.S. Dr. D criticized American clinics using this extreme case to highlight the social disasters caused by the Western approach to technology.

Criticizing the Western approach to technology, Dr. D developed a traditional idea of "following nature" and promoted restraint. The awe she once felt in the face of *Ming* suggests human beings should refrain from abusing their power by exploiting technology. She stressed that "we should follow nature" (*shun qi*

---

[3] Dr. Deng criticized the abuse of technology in the U.S. Indeed the most significant difference between ARTs practise in the U.S. and that in Europe is the regulatory environment (Gleicher et al, 2006). Many practices that are routinely conducted in the U.S. are not allowed in Europe. For example, for a long time, European countries such as France, Austria, and Germany did not allow single women to freeze embryos or use egg donation (German Act, 1990; Bernat and Straka, 1992; Bernat and Vranes, 1993). Germany also stipulates the maximal number of embryos that can be transferred during one treatment cycle. In UK and Sweden, eggs and embryos can only be stored for pre-specified number of years (Human Fertilisation and Embryology Act, 2020; Hamberger and Wikland, 1993).

zi ran). The idea of "following nature" derives from the framework of *Ming*. Here, "nature" (*zi ran*) does not refer to material and physical objects such as the grown environment or organic phenomena. Instead, nature signifies a desirable status in order to cope with *Ming*. In chapter 25 of *Dao De Jing*, a philosophical text authored in the sixth century BCE, Lao Zi wrote that "the human emulates the earthly, the earthly emulates the heavenly, the heavenly emulates the *dao*, the *dao* emulates *zi ran*" (*ren fa di, di fa tian, tian fa dao, dao fa zi ran*)" (Lao, 2010, p.17). *Zi ran*, nature, stands at the summit of this ontological hierarchy. To achieve a state of *zi ran*, Lao Zi explained, the "sage supports all things in their *zi ran* but does not take any action (*sheng ren wu wei er zi ran*)" (2010, p.30). *Zi ran* a state of as-it-isness over which people exert no control. Whether *Ming* brings happiness or adversity, following nature means forsaking all attempts to undo or alter this essential order.

In the process of spiral modernization, reflection prompts shifts in policies. For instance, in the realm of ARTs, my interviewees recognized the boundaries of human influence in reproduction. Consequently, they embraced a return to the traditional principle of following nature, veering away from the over-reliance on modern ART practices. The following nature justifies that ARTs should be conducted in medical conditions. Clinicians believe people should try to conceive without the help of assisted technologies. They can only use ARTs when there are no other options (e.g. when people have infertility diseases). And if fertility treatment still proves unsuccessful, it suggests that *Ming* has not granted these people children. Hence, there is no need for excessive reliance on ARTs. Moreover, when we apply the spiral modernization framework to urbanization, policymakers come to acknowledge its constraints. The following nature explains some counterurbanization measures that the government takes, such as protecting agricultural land, revitalizing rural tourism, and encouraging migrant workers to turn to rural areas for living and operating business. As Chairman Xi spoke at the Sixth Group Study on Ecological Civilization Construction Facilitated by the Political Bureau of the Central Committee of the CPC, "We must establish an ecological civilization strategy whereby we follow nature and adhere to the basic policy of saving resources and protecting the environment" (quoted in Xinhua, 2023).

Returning to Dr. D's criticism of American clinics, I observed the traditional concept of "following nature" promises to affirm a distinct national character that is different from the Western paradigm of using technologies. Dr. D's narratives were wedded to eminently nationalist discourses. Throughout our interview, she frequently condemned American practices, stating, "Clinics in the US often brag about the magic power of their advanced technologies" (Dr. D, 2016c). She also criticized American clinics for prioritizing profit over the appropriate use of fertility treatments. In contrast, the traditional Chinese approach to conception aligns with the heavenly *Ming*, while the American approach tends to exploit technologies. Dr. D recounted how her friend Dr. Y traveled to the United States for sex selection procedures but was unsuccessful in conceiving. Her criticism of the American application of ARTs resonates with the phrase "Chinese Characteristics for the New Era" that policymakers frequently use nowadays to differentiate China's modernization from that of the West. Policymakers take pride in the fact that ancient Chinese wisdom remains relevant in contemporary politics. The integration of the traditional notion of *Ming* into policymaking regarding ARTs suggests that the traditional Chinese approach to technology usage is superior.

Following nature not only holds intrinsic value but also provides extrinsic benefits. Numerous studies have found that failures to conceive are often perceived as solely individual problems, leading to stigma particularly directed at women struggling with infertility (Greil, 2011; Taebi, 2021; Brown, 2022). However, when reproductive outcomes, especially instances where technology "failed" (meaning technology and scientific knowledge could not predict individual outcomes or explain their causes), are attributed to *Ming*, *Ming* appears capable of alleviating the challenges associated with modern technology and its limitations. This can ease the burden on patients. Therefore, *Ming* does not necessarily operate in opposition to science but rather complements it. Yuanhong (2016), for example, told me how she took every measure to avoid having a miscarriage, yet her first pregnancy still failed:

> I did not dare to eat tomatoes and grapes as I was worried about the hormones inside the fruits. My favorite dish was lamb neck hotpot. I did not eat it after pregnancy, as there was Chinese medicine inside the dish. I also did not use laundry powder because it harmed babies. I was hungry and tired every day. Sadly, I still lost my baby.

No matter how hard Yuanhong tried, her precautions could not alter her fate. Studies show personal lifestyles can affect live birth rates of ARTs, and they recommend a few healthy lifestyles to improve ARTs' success rates, such as getting rid of smoking, taking a Mediterranean diet, and maintaining less stressful life (Wang et al., 2000, 2002; Nichols et al., 2003; Hassan and Killick, 2004; Klonoff-Cohen, 2005; Hornstein, 2016; Karayiannis et al, 2018; Aimagambetova et al, 2020). However, in the belief system of *Ming*, outcomes are given in advance, leaving no significant scope for intervention. The second time that she tried fertility treatment, she decided to eat whatever she wanted. "Pregnancy," she said, "is all about *Ming*. I will let nature take its course" (Yuanhong, 2016). Instead of impotently struggling to get pregnant, she reconciled herself to *Ming*.

Sociologists Kuo-Shu Yang and David YF Ho have discussed the psychological advantages of external attribution. *Ming* allows people to "soothe relationships, reduce conflict, and promote social harmony" (1998, p.270). Indeed, Yuanhong described how she could not face her family and friends after losing her first baby. She had blamed herself for losing the baby. Attributing the outcome of her treatment to *Ming* would absolve her of all responsibility. If pregnancy were seen as fateful and uncontrollable, her anxiety would be soothed.

Like Yuanhong, Fuying also felt relieved when she attributed her treatment results to *Ming*. The author met Fuying during a public lecture at the clinic. She was 45 and owned a store. She was diagnosed with ovarian cysts in 2014. Her first round of egg freezing failed. She had almost lost hope before her treatment, she told the author, because she no longer produced enough eggs and no donated eggs were available. She struck lucky, however, in that her eggs were mature. She completed embryo implantation and attended a lecture to gather further information. She agreed that pregnancy depends on *Ming*: "I know that pregnancy is about *Ming*. If you have children in *Ming*, then you will get pregnant anyway. If you do not have children in *Ming*, you will never get pregnant" (Fuying, 2016). This was the reason, she supposed, that she had not yet conceived. As she said, "I did not stay in bed this time. I walk outside and go shopping. I have not closed my business. I eat whatever I want to eat" (Fuying, 2016).

Baoying

Ming undermines human agency. Following *Ming*, however, does not mean ARTs' outcomes are completely irrelevant to human behavior. Patients believed that the influence of human morality on treatment outcomes was so great that no modern technology—including ARTs—could overcome it. I relate Guilan's story to explain that "immorality" will bring adverse effects to fertility treatment. Guilan went to P Clinic with her husband for IVF treatment. Everything went well, but she had to freeze eggs because clinicians were unable to retrieve her husband's sperm on the day of gamete retrieval. She then worried about the outcomes of her fertility treatment. She (2016) attributed the struggles that she faced during her fertility treatment to her previous "immoral" behavior—namely, an abortion:

> I married at 23. If I did not abort my first child, he or she would be going to college this year. I have a friend who also aborted her first child and has been unable to get pregnant since then. This is a real *Baoying* … Do not emulate me. Do not have an abortion. I aborted my child because I was not married and I did not want children in early life. How stupid I was. My mother complained all day, 'If you did not lose your first child,

you will have your second child now.' That is true. It is *Baoying* that my husband's sperm could not be retrieved, and I have not been able to get pregnant. I was already very regretful.

Here, Guilan mentioned the term *Baoying*, which Cynthia Brokaw describes as a "belief in a supernatural or cosmic retribution, a belief that has been a fundamental, at times the fundamental, belief of Chinese religion since the beginning of recorded history" (2014, p.28). In English, the traditional Chinese notion of *Baoying* is often translated into the Buddhist notion of "karmic retribution." Indeed, French sinologist Jacques Gernet has argued that "thanks to certain analogies such as that between *Baoying* and karma, Buddhism was more readily absorbed into Chinese practices of belief" (1982, p.215). *Baoying* is quite different from karma, however. Karma is an individual and spiritual notion (Zhang, 2010). In Guilan's story, by contrast, *Baoying* bears upon secular interests, such as fertility. In addition, it is thought that *Baoying* goes beyond the individual and can be passed down through families and generations. In this instance, it applied not only to Guilan, but to her husband too.

Baoying is the name for the reward or punishment from *Ming*. If individuals behave badly, it is likely that their *Ming* will bring them adversity. Conversely, if individuals behave morally, they will receive a fortune. Accordingly, *Ming* resembles a court set up to judge social morality, reward virtue, and punish evil. The idea of *Baoying* implies that people dwell in a moral universe. As such, the notion of *Baoying* has similarities with the theory of moral fate put forward by Sinian Fu. "The theory that *Ming* rectifies," Fu explains, "held that the affections of heaven were not constant, and that conduct toward others could bring down good fortune or calamity" (1952, p.16). Whether people behave in favor of *Ming* influences the outcomes of their behaviors. The Chinese philosopher Ning Chen has also addressed the morality of the *Ming*. He distinguishes between two separate meanings of *Ming*, both of which can exist simultaneously. On the one hand, *Ming* means blind fate. Events are fixed in advance and cannot be altered by human agency. On the other, it refers to moral determinism, according to which "happiness and misery are determined by a moral and personal god who oversees human social and ethical conduct, rewarding the good and punishing the wicked" (1997, p.495). Whereas the unpredictable and uncontrollable aspect of *Ming* discussed in the previous two sections belongs to the category of blind fate, the dimension of moral determinism described in this section can serve to explain Guilan's experience. Guilan believed she was punished for abortion. Infertility and failed treatment, then, represented the *Baoying* (punishment) imposed on Guilan and her husband.

Moral conduct can bring about rewards; immoral conduct can give rise to adversity. Indeed, Guilan hoped that her *Ming* could be put right by showing remorse. People often rely on various forms of mantic knowledge and practices of exorcism to reinforce their good behavior. For instance, many Chinese people regularly visit temples to pray for wealth, health, and happiness. As the American Sinologist Daniel Overmyer observes, "Chinese local rituals and beliefs are similar to those of ordinary people in many other cultures, whatever their larger political and intellectual contexts; wherever one looks, one sees people praying and sacrificing to their gods or saints for help in dealing with the difficulties of life, appeals that can also involve festivals and processions" (2008, p.178). When I met Ruiying, she was in the waiting lounge showing other patients how her Buddhist amulet had helped her get pregnant. Although she had not officially "converted" to Buddhism, she wore a Buddhist amulet every day. A monk told her that the amulet would show her kindness and hence would help her succeed in fertility treatment. Indeed, vendors selling Buddha beads and statues were popular near P Clinic. Begging business also prospered. Sometimes, I encountered a few beggars asking for money in one day. Patients purchased Buddha beads or helped beggars not solely out of altruism but to help fulfill their wishes.

The moral side of *Ming* suggests that it differs from the Western idea of fate. *Ming* encompasses two interconnected yet distinct meanings: fixed fate and moral decree, whereas fate does not. The moral aspect of *Ming* compels individuals to adhere to social norms—the heavenly responsibilities that individuals are expected to fulfill. Failure to fulfill these duties may result in adverse consequences, known as bad *Baoying*. Therefore, while the fixed fate aspect of *Ming* alleviates the burden on patients and doctors by discouraging endless reliance on ARTs, the moral aspect of *Ming* is not necessarily comforting. Throughout my research, I discovered that moral norms, particularly regarding women's reproductive lives, were utilized to further state policy agendas such as population growth.

Ming forbids women from having abortions. Guilan's experience of abortion, for example, diminished her confidence in treatment. She believed that her abortion incurred bad *Baoying*. She believed that her husband was also being punished for it, even though there was no verifiable link between her abortion and his inability to retrieve sperm. Similarly, one day, a woman almost fainted upon learning that her embryo had stopped growing. Dr. D explained to her that the endometrium had damaged the embryo. Despite Dr. D's reassurances that she had frozen additional embryos, the woman lost hope. "I had an abortion before," she said (source anonymized, 2016a). "It is *Baoying*. No technology can save me" (source anonymized, 2016a). She believed that her infertility was a punishment for her abortion, and medical treatment couldn't prevent such punishments. Although she had frozen embryos for future treatments, she feared they might also fail due to the punishment.

In China, abortion was once legal at all stages of pregnancy and widely accessible nationwide. Abortion advertisements can be found on buses, TVs, and street walls. Aligned with the now-defunct One-Child Policy, the government provided universal access to abortion to control the population. Today, some hospitals still offer abortion services under the Department for Family Planning. In 2022, to increase the country's birth rate, the National Health Commission (NHC) announced measures to reduce non-medically necessary abortions. The reflection on the declining birth rate and the reversal of abortion policies reflect the dynamics of a spiral society in which policy adjustments respond to evolving contexts. However, I need to acknowledge that China's commitment to limiting abortions still places women's bodies under state control, akin to the One-Child Policy, and could stigmatize women who have had abortions. The stigmas surrounding abortion during my fieldwork reflect the government's evolving stance on abortion. As abortion becomes morally contentious, women are encouraged to choose childbirth.

In addition to abortions, my interviewees believed *Ming* discourages late childbearing. Guilan believed that her niece was being punished for marrying and attempting to have children later in life. She (2016) even equated late childbearing with abortions, arguing that both would result in bad *Baoying*:

> My niece is already 29. She has obtained a graduate degree. She now works in a hospital in Shanghai with a monthly salary of ¥10,000. She was single for a long time and declined blind dates. Now, she is married but does not have children. This is her *Baoying* … Although you are young, you should marry and conceive children in early life.

Guilan attributed her niece's childlessness to her decision to marry and attempt to have children later in life despite being only 29 years old. Guilan saw the late postponement of having children as immoral: a violation of *Ming*. Had her niece married and conceived children in early life, she would not have been punished with childlessness. Hence, she cautioned me not to delay childbearing because she believed that late childbearing would lead to punishment.

The clinicians also applied the traditional idea of *Baoying* to encourage women to conceive children in early life. An article shared on P Clinic's WeChat platform, for example, warned women that if they failed to conceive children in early life, then they might become infertile:

> Age is the major factor. The loss of ovarian functions is irreversible. No technology can treat aging. The older women get, the poorer their egg

quality and the higher the miscarriage rate ... friends, do not consider egg freezing. If you want to get pregnant, do not be too late. Your ovaries cannot wait, regardless of egg freezing. Otherwise, you will get stuck in a situation of childlessness. This is your *Baoying*. You will regret that you did not follow your *Ming*. You will regret your decision on egg freezing. Although we treat infertile women, we wish that every woman would get pregnant naturally and prevent infertility (source anonymized, 2015).

According to the article, no technologies, including egg freezing, can reverse aging, for aging is a bodily rule. The only way to prevent age-related fertility decline is to conceive children in early life. Furthermore, the article stresses that even if some women freeze eggs to postpone childbearing, their outcomes will not necessarily be positive. It warns that, ultimately, such women will fail to get pregnant. Childlessness is bad *Baoying*—women's punishment for not conceiving children when they should. This article sheds light on why age-related fertility decline is not included as one of the indications for the medical use of ARTs. The rationale behind the regulations is to adhere to *Ming*'s advice, which suggests that healthy individuals should not postpone childbearing. Waiting until fertility declines and then pursuing fertility treatment as an alternative means of conceiving children goes against this advice. Therefore, there is no need to utilize fertility preservation technologies such as egg freezing for preventive purposes.

The promotion of early childbearing is gendered, which explains why men (and even single men) are allowed to preserve sperm for social or family purposes. Clinicians explained that the legitimacy of women's early childbearing is rooted in the inherent differences between men and women. For instance, according to Dr. D, men and women have distinct bodily structures. While women undergo menopause, men do not. Despite age affecting men's reproductive abilities, men can still produce sperm and father children in their 50s and beyond. In contrast, menopause signifies that women's ovaries no longer produce functioning eggs. Hence, Dr. D argues, the countdown to the onset of menopause requires that women conceive children in early life. Dr. Z, another fertility specialist working at P Clinic, also invoked menopause to urge women to conceive children in early life. The links that clinicians made between women's bodily structure and their moral responsibilities almost constitute a form of essentialism. Among the clinicians, bodily differences between the two sexes were regarded as sacred rules that determine gender norms.[4] To them, women's bodies dictate what women should and should not do, what is worthy and unworthy. Women were created

[4] Sex beyond the binary is formed through fetal development.

in such a way that they are supposed to experience fertility decline and menopause. They should, therefore, follow these heavenly rules.

This study reveals the intense efforts to regulate women's reproductive age. Guilan's niece, at 29 years old, was already considered late for childbearing. Clinicians warned that age-related fertility decline served as a punishment for women who delayed childbearing. These perspectives resonate with the reflection on the constraints associated with delayed marriage and childbirth, which was advocated by Chairman Deng and the subsequent policy reversals which illustrate the ongoing process of spiral modernization. For example, attitudes toward egg freezing have significantly shifted. As mentioned in Chapter 1, initially, the government encouraged women to preserve their fertility through egg freezing. However, clinicians in this study discouraged women from pursuing egg freezing, arguing that it is a woman's responsibility to marry and conceive children early in life. They cautioned that deviating from this normative path could result in negative consequences, such as bad *Baoying*.

Legislator Y concurred with the clinicians' arguments regarding adherence to bodily laws. He (2016) introduced that in 2015, the government no longer adhered to the view that "family planning is the fundamental national policy" (to use Legislator Y's own words). "Nowadays, the demographic dividend is decreasing," he (2016) said. "Women should obey their biological laws and conceive children in early life. Delayed childbearing is harmful" (Legislator Y, 2016). While clinicians cited *Ming* and *Baoying* as supernatural forces influencing pregnancy and childbearing, it is evident that authorities such as clinicians and policymakers determine what ages are deemed appropriate for childbearing. Supernatural forces were invoked to encourage women to adhere to policy agendas rather than pursue their own reproductive plans.

Summary

The chapter explored skepticism around ARTs as a path toward successful procreation. Both the clinicians and the patients in this study adhered to a traditional Chinese concept, *Ming*, which governs the course of human lives, including reproduction. *Ming* signifies one's unpredictable, unapproachable, and uncontrollable destiny. According to this belief, the success of ARTs is determined by a patient's destiny, which modern technology cannot alter. Since the outcomes of ARTs are uncertain, individuals are advised to adhere to nature's rules and refrain from using technology to manipulate their destinies. Clinicians, therefore, only administer fertility treatment to address medical conditions such as infertility. When patients are capable of conceiving naturally, ARTs are not recommended. The traditional belief in *Ming* serves to disenchant modern technology, fostering an awareness of the importance of not abusing it. The interviewees repackaged this traditional belief in contemporary society to distinguish Chinese approaches to technology from Western methods.

Moreover, *Baoying*—the further concept in *Ming*'s philosophical framework —rests on the idea that *Ming* rewards or punishes individuals in relation to their morality. Despite the absence of a direct scientific link between human morality and reproduction outcomes, my interviewees believed that immoral behavior may lead to adversity, such as failed fertility treatment. Consequently, individuals must adhere to social, moral, and heavenly rules to realize their hopes. Immoral behavior, as perceived by the interviewees, included abortion and delayed childbearing. Therefore, the clinicians did not consider age-related fertility decline in women as a legitimate medical reason, as they believed delayed childbearing violates women's bodily rules and may result in bad *Baoying*. The interviewees underscored the traditional belief in *Baoying* as a response to the fertility decline in China.

This chapter examined my interviewees' reflections on uncertain outcomes of ARTs, highlighting the influence of reflection in driving policy reversals. Policy reflections and reversals are notable characteristics of spiral modernization. This chapter outlined policy reversals based on the traditional idea of *Ming*, such as the restraint of ARTs to prevent technology misuse and the promotion of early childbearing to curb fertility decline. The next chapter will explain the rationale behind the controversial marriage-related access criteria for ARTs. It will analyze how my interviewees revisited the traditional concept of paternal uncertainty in light of social open-up in China.

Chapter 4

Paternal uncertainty

However, a distinction in English common law arose in respect of a child
born to unmarried parents. At common law, an illegitimate child was
filius nullius, the son of no one, or *fillius populi*, the son of the people.
——Gubernat v. Deremer, 1995

Genetic paternal uncertainty

In Chapter 3, I explained ARTs are limited in medical conditions due to
uncertain outcomes caused by *Ming* rather than low success rates. I also
explained why clinicians do not view women's age-related infertility as a
legitimate medical reason for conducting ARTs. In this chapter, I will explore
why the regulations set women's marriage status as one of the conditions to
access ARTs.

At first glance, the condition of women's marriage seems unnecessary. On the
one hand, outcomes of technologies are irrelevant to marital status. On the
other hand, there is no similar restriction for single men. Then why is women's
marriage status so important? This question bears upon a surprising case that
was brought before an ethics committee of P Clinic during my fieldwork.[1] A 21-
year-old single woman experienced early menopause. The debate concerned
whether the clinic should freeze her eggs, allowing her to use them in the future.
The woman showed a clear medical indication. However, for clinicians, the
case was complex, involving a number of possible scenarios that deserved
detailed discussion. Therefore, they passed the case to the ethics committee.
Surprisingly, the ethics committee rejected the woman's request because she

---

[1] A qualified committee should have at least seven members. More than one third of these
members should be external to the clinic. In addition, committee members should be
trained in a variety of disciplines, including biology, medicine, law, and sociology,
although the opinions of medical specialists are also necessary (Yu et al,2015 p.2). A
reproductive medical ethics committee is an independent organization operating within
a clinic. It supervises ARTs practices according to regulations laid down by the Ministry
of Health, educates patients and clinicians about ARTs ethics, evaluates and approves
new technologies, and deals with ethical issues.

had not had sexual intercourse and that egg retrieval would damage her hymen.

This case reveals two rationales for whether a fertility treatment request can be approved. First, medical indications are not the only prerequisites for using ARTs. There is a hierarchy among different prerequisites. In this case, marital status overrode the woman's medical condition. Second, clinicians take women's sexual experiences into account. The ethics committee denied the woman's request, it would seem, not only because she was unmarried but also because she was still a virgin.

My findings from observing Dr. D's consultation room echoed the case. For unmarried women seeking fertility treatment, it appeared that clinicians would consider their treatment requests if they showed medical indications and had sexual experience.[2] For example, Yufen came to Dr. D to fertilize her frozen eggs because she just gotten married and was ready to conceive a child. She froze eggs in P Clinic in 2010 after being diagnosed with Polycystic ovary syndrome (PCOS). Given that she was unmarried, clinicians did not recommend embryo freezing, which can produce higher success rates than egg freezing. In light of the fact that she already had sex with her boyfriend, clinicians allowed her to freeze eggs.

Why does sex experience matter in fertility treatment? Clinicians regarded women's fertility treatment to be invasive, involving the insertion of devices into a woman's vagina. Whether it's egg retrieval or embryo implantation, vaginal penetration is unavoidable. For a woman who is a virgin, this penetration may damage her hymen.

According to Dr. W, such penetration "will transform single women's unmarried vaginas into married vaginas" (Dr. W, 2016). Here, Dr. W drew two comparisons. First, she equated single women with virgin women. She assumed that single women are meant to be virgins. Second, she equated medical penetration with sexual penetration. A needle entering a women's vagina was compared to a penis being inserted into a woman's body. By suggesting that medical devices could take a single woman's virginity through vaginal penetration, Dr. W uses the term "penetration" to describe the insertion of medical devices into a single woman's body. In Chinese, the term for

---

[2] I do not know if it is only sexually experienced unmarried women diagnosed with Polycystic ovary syndrome (PCOS) who can freeze their eggs; the two women I encountered were both diagnosed with PCOS. When I asked Dr. D about the medical criteria that suggest that egg freezing would be appropriate, she said that they include PCOS, menopause, and tubal obstruction. Nevertheless, she emphasized that single women's cases would be subject to review by the ethics committee.

penetration (*cha ru*) could imply sexual intercourse, mirroring a similar linguistic parallel as in English.

Similarly, Dr. D also claimed the transvaginal method of egg retrieval will break a hymen if it is still intact at the time of an operation. In fact, according to Dr. D, the primary reason why the regulations do not posit marriage as a prerequisite for freezing sperm is the fact that "sperm freezing is not invasive, while egg freezing is invasive" (Dr. D, 2016c). Dr. D (2016c) explained:

> Young men will enjoy peace of mind after they freeze sperm. We clinicians welcome young men who want to freeze sperm. … In China and in many countries, egg freezing is not allowed. Egg freezing penetrates women's bodies. It is invasive.

Dr. D concluded that egg freezing has to penetrate women's bodies, while sperm freezing does not invade men's bodies. Indeed, for men with normal sperm production, to retrieve sperm, they can ejaculate semen consciously. Even surgical sperm retrieval, which inserts a needle into testicles and aspirates sperm, does not impact men's virginity. On the contrary, during egg retrieval, a long thin needle fixed on a probe of a thin vaginal ultrasound is placed into the vagina. Hymen, a symbol of virginity, will easily be scratched or injured.

In routine clinical practices, in addition to ARTs, gynecological examinations of unmarried women were cautioned—unless the women in question were no longer virgins. When I interviewed two members of staff in the egg-freezing agencies, they both mentioned the embarrassment surrounding the gynecological examination (including transvaginal tests) of unmarried women. Miss Zhang (2017), manager at C egg freezing agency, stressed that "women need to provide marriage certificates and birth certificates in order to get treatment in the gynecology departments of public hospitals, but only married women have marriage certificates and birth certificates." Miss Yang (2016), a member of staff at O egg freezing agency, said that she "asked [her] clients to tell clinicians frankly that they had sex before and want to have a gynecological examination. Most clinicians will not decline their request."

The medical penetration of ARTs could damage the hymen, traditionally seen as an indicator of virginity, leading single women to feel as though they have engaged in premarital sex. The clinicians' metaphor of penetration emphasizes that women should remain virgins until marriage. The loss of virginity before marriage is a significant concern, particularly for men. Dr. D told me a story about an unmarried woman whose hymen was accidentally broken during a gynecological examination. Despite the fact that the woman's hymen was only affected by medical equipment, her boyfriend doubted her fidelity and decided to end the relationship. Dr. D explained, "Even though we all know the woman's hymen was accidentally broken, her boyfriend did not believe. He asserted that she had had sex with another man" (Dr. D, 2016c). To avoid such disputes, clinicians refrain from inserting devices into the vaginas of single women. If the widespread use of ARTs among single women were allowed, clinicians could be held responsible for damaging the hymens of virgin women. As Dr. D emphasized, "Clinicians should be very careful when they treat single women. We cannot arouse men's concerns" (Dr. D, 2016c).

The link between premarital loss of virginity and men's doubts about women's fidelity stems from an ancient belief known as "paternal uncertainty." Before the invention of DNA paternity tests, only women were certain that the children they carried were genetically related to them; the fact that fertilization occurs inside women, however, meant that men were often uncertain as to the paternity of their children (Trivers, 1972). Fathers were, therefore, less inclined to provide optimal care for their offspring (Gilding, 2009). Throughout history, men developed various strategies to ensure their genetic relationship with their children. These strategies included chastity belts; female genital modifications, such as infibulation; preventing women from communicating with men; limiting women's mobility by binding their feet; forcing women to cover themselves with robes and veils (Wilson and Daly, 1992; Potts and Roger, 1999). Preference for chaste mates is one of the male psyche's paternal assurance tactics (Platek and Shackelford, 2006). Fidelity in women decreases the likelihood of conceiving children with other men during marriage, thus safeguarding the genetic relationship between husbands and children. Studies have shown that males experience significant anxiety when considering their wives' potential infidelity, and confirmation of adultery often leads to relationship termination (D. M. Buss et al., 1992; Shackelford et al., 2002). In Dr. D's anecdote, the woman's boyfriend doubted her fidelity and immediately ended their relationship upon learning of her loss of virginity before marriage, even though it did not involve "real" sexual intercourse.

Similar to the preference for chaste wives, the restriction of single women's access to ARTs represents an attempt to seal the womb. The restriction constitutes a symbolic mate-guarding strategy to allay genetic paternal uncertainty. It seeks to ensure that single women's virginity remains unquestioned, reassuring future husbands about their wives' fidelity and their children's lineage. Consequently, the criteria limiting access to ARTs based on women's marital status primarily serve men's interests, despite claims of protecting women's virginity made by my interviewees.

Women's premarital virginity was deemed to be important in ancient China. As Song philosopher named Yi Chen recommended, "if a noble man marries a non-virgin woman, he loses his own social status" (*Ruo qu shi jie zhe yi pei shen, shi ji shi jie ye*) (quoted in Rosenlee 2007, p.132). The vigorous promotion of the idea that brides should remain virgins consolidated the idea that prior sexual experience ruled women out as legitimate potential mates. This emphasis on chastity was enforced rigorously, with girls from noble families prohibited from freely interacting with men before marriage. Punishments for premarital sex could be severe, such as being thrown into a pig cage as a consequence of losing one's virginity.

However, with the opening up of Chinese society in the 1980s, attitudes toward premarital sex began to shift. As mentioned in Chapter 2, many women now feel more comfortable expressing their sexual desires, viewing sex as a source of pleasure rather than solely for procreation. Consequently, the notion of paternal certainty has been challenged. In contemporary society, advancements like DNA testing allow men to confirm their biological relationship with children regardless of their partners' sexual history before marriage. However, I argue that paternal uncertainty in this context is more symbolic than actual, representing men's feelings of anxiety or confusion upon learning about their partners' premarital sexual experiences.

Paternal uncertainty can be seen as a reflection of the liberal attitudes towards premarital sex. In response to this challenge, policymakers emphasize conservative norms of sexual morality for women, representing a policy reversal within the context of spiral modernization. According to Official H (2017) from the NHFPC,

> even though the Constitution entitles people to equal reproduction rights, we still think that sex and reproduction should only occur within marriage. Love without marriage is Eros, but love within marriage is Vesta (*yi qie bu yi jie hun wei mu di de tan lian ai dou shi shua liu mang*).

For Official H, sex outside marriage is driven by pleasure, while sex inside marriage is sacred. Official H's perspective resonates with the traditional cultural teachings on virginity imparted through courses for Good Women in the New Era, as discussed in Chapter 2. This educational approach struck a chord with me, as it brought to mind the sex education I received during my sophomore year in 2012. The textbook set for the course *Human Beings' Sex, Reproduction, and Health* contains the following passage:

> When women have sex with other men before marriage, millions of sperm enter into women's bodies. Some of them are autolyzed. When sperm are autolyzed, they release a genetic material called ribosome, which can be absorbed by the inner glands of the female reproductive organs. Semen also contains a variety of sex hormones which can also be absorbed by women. Sperm which are absorbed by women's body as

well as DNA mutate and assimilate women's sex cells. Therefore, women could conceive children who not only bear their husbands' DNA but also the DNA of those guys who have had sex with them. (Chen, 2005, p. 27)

This passage teaches women to maintain their virginity until marriage, citing the prolonged presence of men's genetic cells in the vagina during sexual intercourse as a reason. The underlying argument is that preserving premarital virginity helps mitigate paternal uncertainty by reducing the likelihood of women conceiving children with sperm from men other than their eventual husbands. This, in turn, ensures that husbands can be confident about the genetic lineage of their offspring. While this argument may be contentious and outdated, what is particularly striking is its inclusion in a twenty-first-century science textbook. This underscores the persistence of the age-old belief in "paternal uncertainty" and its influence on contemporary discourse. In her classic essay Sperm and Eggs, Emily Martin (1991) argues that rather than dispel gender myths, scientific texts reproduce gendered ideologies. Similarly, this textbook justifies and reinforces norms on women's chastity with scientific evidence, which is actually an extension of the traditional expression of men's reproductive drive.

Many women internalize such sexual morality norms. During my research, I encountered a woman in the clinic who attributed her infertility to having lost her virginity before marriage. She expressed regret, stating, "Once women become women before marriage, they easily suffer from gynecological disease, which causes infertility. This is my *Baoying*. I really feel regretful" (source anonymized, 2016b). Here, the phrase "becoming a woman" refers to sexual intercourse and the loss of virginity. She felt so embarrassed about having lost her virginity before getting married that she used this obscure euphemism. She believed that her infertility was a punishment for her premarital sexual activity.

Legal Paternity

The previous section discusses the concept of paternal uncertainty in traditional evolutionary psychology, where men cannot confirm paternity without DNA testing. According to my interviewees, prohibiting single women—who are expected to be virgins—from using ARTs serves as a mate-guarding strategy. In this section, I delve into how legal paternity is established in fertility treatments where genetic paternity is absent, such as sperm donation.

The development of ARTs has given rise to new ways of defining both maternal and paternal relationships (Franklin, 2013). Maternity, for instance, is not so obvious in cases of a gestational mother bearing a child and another, a genetic mother supplies the egg. The *Book* raises an example of egg restructuring (Yu et al., 2015, p.20). The technology revives aging eggs by implanting a young woman's ovoplasm into the eggs of an older woman. After that, the older woman must find a surrogate to conceive the child or children. Consequently, the older woman's eggs will contain the young woman's DNA, and the surrogate will deliver the child or children. In this case, children born with the help of egg restructuring will have three mothers (if that is, we chose to define maternal relationships by reference to bio-genetic facts). Paternity is similarly challenged in the case of sperm donation: the man who provides sperm and the man who raises the child are two different people.

When children are born using ARTs, who are their parents? Perhaps biological evidence is not best positioned to answer the question. Several factors might be brought to bear on this question: the mother's marital status, the sperm recipient's relationship with the mother, and the sperm donor's identity. Each of these criteria, rather than biology, may be taken to identify the parents. Therefore, instead of simply sweeping away old genetic definitions of parenthood and replacing them with a new, biogenetic one, reproductive technologies have actually heightened the tensions between multiple criteria for defining parenthood.

In any case, "Who are the parents?" might not be the right question. A better one, perhaps, is: how does society—including its legal and political systems—establish parentage? To grasp how parentage is formulated legally in China, I interviewed Legislator Y from the NPC and read relevant legal documents. Deciding who a child's legal parents are is no easy task, especially when children are born with the help of ARTs. According to Legislator Y, instinctively, one would point to the child's biological parents. However, in the situation of ARTs, sometimes clear-cut rules do not apply.

Chinese law treats deliverers rather than egg providers as legal mothers. It comes to the fore when the *Book* raises the issue of egg donation (Yu et al., 2015, p. 211). Egg donors provide genetic elements, while legal mothers provide wombs and raise children. Although there is a genetic relationship between egg donors and children, the law does not identify egg donors as legal mothers but as those who provide wombs. My findings attest to the power of what the legal scholar Yuan Zhang has called a "birth fact" (2005), which emphasizes how pregnancy establishes a close relationship between mother and child. Another practice discussed in the *Book* is that of surrogacy, whereby a woman provides eggs and then finds a surrogate to deliver a child or children (Yu et al., 2015, p. 20). By undertaking surrogacy, the egg provider hopes to become the child or children's mother. As the deliverer, however, the surrogate is the legal mother. According to the *Book*, "surrogacy contravenes the current legal framework, according to which a legal mother delivers children" (Yu et al., 2015, p.116).

Given that surrogacy raises the challenging question of whether a birth mother is, in fact, a legal mother, the Chinese government has banned surrogacy.

Whereas maternity is defined by a single principle called "birth fact," the paternity of children born through ARTs is defined case by case. In a legal document concerning paternity, "The Legal Status of the Children who are Born from Artificial Insemination after Couples Divorce," which the Supreme Court produced in 1991, the document presents judicial interpretations of a divorce case. The case involves Mr. Yang and Ms. Wang, who married in December 1987. After Mr. Yang was diagnosed with Azoospermia in their first year of marriage, Ms. Wang underwent artificial insemination with donor sperm in 1989, resulting in the birth of their daughter. In 1990, Ms. Wang filed for divorce, and Mr. Yang contested paying for their daughter's expenses, claiming no genetic relationship. However, the Supreme Court ruled Mr. Yang as the legal father and obligated him to provide financial support for two reasons: the child was born during their marriage, and Mr. Yang implicitly consented to the insemination procedure by being present at the clinic and participating in raising the child.

This judgment underscores that sperm donors are solely biological fathers without any legal ties to the children. Moreover, it establishes marriage and consent as pivotal factors in determining legal paternity. The court's emphasis on "the child was born while the couple was married" indicates that marriage supersedes biological ties in establishing legal fatherhood (Supreme Court, 1991). Essentially, marriage takes precedence over biology in matters of legal paternity.

Furthermore, the court indicates that the man in question should acknowledge his daughter's paternity because he did not oppose it during the artificial insemination process. Had his wife used donor sperm without his consent, he could have legitimately disavowed fatherhood. The judicial interpretation stresses the importance of consent in situations of sperm donation, "When married couples use donated sperm if husbands accept sperm donation, husbands are legal fathers of children. Without husbands' agreement, husbands can deny legal fatherhood" (Supreme Court, 1991). In other words, husbands who consent to sperm donation are legally recognized as fathers according to the law (Chen, 2009).

Accepting sperm donation in China is not easy. In their book *Transforming Patriarchy: Chinese Families in the Twenty-First Century* (2017), Stevan Harrell and Gonçalo D. Santos explain that Chinese men are unwilling to use donated sperm due to the deeply entrenched tradition of patrilineal kinship in China. In ancient Chinese society, Confucianism emphasized descent traced solely through male lineage. Men who lacked biological offspring were seen as violating filial piety, a cornerstone of Confucian moral values. An old Confucian proverb encapsulates this sentiment: there are three unfilial things that are not filial, and the descendant is the greatest (*bu xiao you san, wu hou wei da*). The *Book* also mentions this:

> Traditional Chinese belief holds that women's chastity and childbirth are indispensable for maintaining a happy marriage and family.......
> Some people think that sperm donation blasphemes against loyal love and even compare it with adultery (Yu et al., 2015, p.99).

Drawing a parallel between sperm donation and adultery, the *Book* argues that both disrupt the father-child relationship. Given that adultery is heavily stigmatized and morally condemned in Chinese society, the same sentiment extends to sperm donation.

Consequently, in clinical practices, clinicians do not recommend sperm donation if there are other options. For example, they freeze eggs for married women seeking fertility treatment when their husbands' sperm is unavailable or unqualified during treatment, even though embryo freezing has higher success rates than egg freezing. This practice resembles what some scholars have termed "incidental egg freezing," in which women freeze eggs during an IVF cycle because fertilization is not complete on the day of egg collection (Gürtin et al. 2019a; Gürtin et al. 2019b). Incidental egg freezing allows husbands to spend time on their treatment in the knowledge that they can have their own children in the future and avoid resorting to sperm donation.

Consider the case of Yanying, who conducted IVF at P Clinic. Clinicians could not retrieve her husband's sperm; they, therefore, froze her eggs. Yanying was adamant about egg freezing to ensure unequivocally that any child born would be biologically related to her husband. "I never considered sperm donation," she told me. "A child who is born from donated sperm would not belong to my husband" (Yanying, 2016). During my fieldwork, I encountered another woman, Yuzhi, who was from Hebei Province. She had got married two months before we met in August 2016. She looked forward to her grand wedding ceremony. Both she and her husband had undergone medical examinations before marriage, revealing that her husband had a genetic disorder. Despite uncertainty regarding her husband's treatment timeline or the prospects of a cure, Yuzhi (2016) remained steadfast in her decision to freeze her eggs at P Clinic, saying:

I did not know that my husband had a genetic disease until we conducted a premarital examination (*hun jian*).[3] I am now waiting for his treatment. In order to get pregnant, we have no choice but to do IVF later. In case I will retrieve the eggs in the future, I want the clinic to have my young eggs and freeze them. I do not know how long my husband's treatment will take. Egg freezing will comfort me and my husband.

When I asked Yuzhi why they had not chosen sperm donation (after all, it was her husband who had a genetic disease), she said she wanted to have her husband's children. Her view of egg freezing as a source of "comfort" suggested that it assuaged her husband's anxieties about the prospect of not fathering his own offspring. In this regard, egg freezing not only affords Yuzhi the opportunity to safeguard her fertility but also preserves her husband's potential to have biological children in the future.

This linkage between incidental egg freezing and legal paternity broadens the perspective put forward by existing studies, which emphasize how egg freezing preserves single women's fertility. According to Lauren Jade Martin, for example:

Egg freezing merely preserves the ability to have a genetically related child. The very meaning of fertility (and, in turn, infertility) is redefined to emphasize the genetic connection. This genetic connection is reified as the gold standard of motherhood, circularly highlighting the necessity to address anticipated infertility by such measures as egg freezing (2010, p.11).

Likewise, Carroll and Charlotte (2017) interviewed 16 women from the Midwest and East Coast regions of the USA, finding that they froze eggs so as to have genetically related healthy babies. It is true that egg freezing allows single women to have genetically related children in the future. Yanying and Yuzhi's experiences, however, indicate that married women in China freeze eggs specifically to avoid sperm donation and safeguard their husbands' prospects of having genetically related children.

In fact, legal paternity is so crucial that when single women who still plan to get married in the future choose among fertility preservation options, embryo freezing (to be used with donated sperm) is the least desirable option, even though embryo freezing produces higher success rates than egg freezing. They

---

[3] Premarital examination checks hereditary illness and diseases that might negatively influence parenting capabilities, such as psychiatric problems. The government abolished mandatory premarital examination in 2003.

choose egg freezing rather than embryo freezing or adoption in order to prevent potential future husbands from disclaiming fatherhood. Let's revisit the case of Yufen, who froze eggs in P Clinic in 2010 after being diagnosed with PCOS. Clinicians did not recommend embryo freezing because she was unmarried. Without a husband to provide consent for the use of donated sperm to fertilize her eggs, embryo freezing wasn't a viable option. Some may wonder if she could have used her boyfriend's sperm. However, considering the possibility of a breakup and subsequent marriage to someone else, her future husband might still contest paternity.

Miss Zhang from C Agency observed that sometimes clinicians recommended that single women conduct embryo freezing using donated sperm, depending on their age. Nevertheless, some of Miss Zhang's clients still preferred to spend money on egg freezing, even though their clinicians told them that their chances of success would be only 10%. My interview with Caifeng, a 40-year-old woman who had a consultation about egg freezing at P Clinic, also indicated why single women prefer egg freezing. Clinicians working at P Clinic told Caifeng that her options were limited because her hormone levels were very low. She could either wait until donated eggs became available or opt for adoption. Regardless, she refused to consider either egg donation or adoption. Regretfully, she (2016) told me that,

> I am not ready for children who are not genetically related to me. … And if I marry in later life, I bet my future husband would not be ready either. I read Jinglei Xu's Weibo. She was over 40 years old, but she still stood a chance of conceiving her own children with the help of egg freezing.

Caifeng did not give up on the idea of marriage. And she believed her future husband would not accept a child who was genetically unrelated to him. This is why Caifeng ruled out sperm donation and adoption. In this sense, the underlying reason that many single women in China plan to freeze eggs is not only that they wish to realize their own reproductive autonomy but also that they want their future husbands to accept their children. As Lisa Schuman, Georgia Witkin, Kira Copperman, and MacDonald Acosta-La Greca claim, "egg freezing is a treatment option for single women who would like to retain some opportunity to parent a genetically related child with a future partner" (2011, p.339). Egg freezing, first and foremost, serves to ensure that these single women's future husbands accept fatherhood. In this sense, the choice between egg freezing and embryo freezing has not only medical dimensions, but social and cultural aspects too.

In cases in which sperm donation is the only viable option, clinicians take measures to facilitate men's acceptance of sperm donation. According to the

Regulations on Human-Assisted Technologies and Sperm Banks, sperm donors' information is to remain confidential, and sperm donors should know neither the sperm recipients nor clinicians. This serves to minimize ambiguity in the relationship between children and sperm donors. In addition, as required by the *Book*, "sperm banks select sperm donors who resemble sperm recipients in terms of their eyes, skin color, height, and other variables" (Yu et al., 2015, p.116). Steven M. Platek and Todd K. Shackelford use the term "paternity assessment" to describe the ways in which men seek to establish paternity by assessing the degree to which a child resembles themselves (2006). As the passage of the *Book* that I have just quoted suggests, men often take facial resemblance to signify paternity. This is supported by many studies. For example, a survey of 151 Chinese kindergarten students' parents indicates that fathers paid more attention to facial similarity with children than mothers; facial resemblance cemented the relationship between fathers and children (Yu et al., 2019). Willfully or not, seeking out sperm donors whose faces resemble those of sperm recipients represents an attempt to manipulate reproduction so as to ensure deeper connections between offspring and sperm recipients. In this practice, the bio-genetic aspects of kinship are brought in symbolically as a paternity metaphor to increase the value and legitimacy of legal paternal relationships in a context in which genetic relationships are absent.

If single women use ARTs to conceive children, they will become single mothers (e.g., through sperm donation). In China, single motherhood also applies to lesbian couples since homosexual marriage is not legal. Both elements of legal paternity in China— marriage and consent—are absent in cases of single motherhood. When single women conceive children, no husbands can act as their legal fathers. In 2017, an NPC deputy proposed liberalizing single women's access to ARTs. In response to the proposal, the former National Health and Family Planning Commission (NHFPC) (2017) said,

> China's legal system is not yet complete, and the restriction of assisted reproductive technology for single women wholly reflects the protection of children's rights. If single women fertilize their eggs with donated sperm, we cannot verify who the children's fathers are.

This passage demonstrates that the government is concerned that if single women conceive children using donated sperm, it is difficult to establish legal paternity.

Moreover, if single women use donated sperm to get pregnant, they are unable to obtain their husbands' consent. If single women with children born in this way marry later in their lives, their future husbands who do not consent to sperm donation could deny the legal paternity of their children. This sheds light on why Jilin Province asks single women to swear that they will not marry in the future before they use ARTs. Although children born through these methods will still lack legal fathers, if single mothers do not marry, then no further family disputes will arise.

After all, single women's use of ARTs to conceive children exacerbates the difficulties of identifying legal paternity. The difficulty of identifying legal paternal relationships within single motherhood represents another kind of paternal uncertainty. As Dr. D (2016c) put it, "The children of single mothers experience a unique form of paternal absence." This absence differs from the genetic form of paternal uncertainty in an evolutionary sense. Genetic paternal uncertainty is psychological. It refers to husbands' anxiety about their partners' loss of virginity. In situations of single motherhood, by contrast, the legal identity of the father is unknown—a vacuum. Unlike mothers who must raise children on their own because fathers have fled their responsibilities, single motherhood through ARTs does not prescribe paternal roles.

In order to mitigate legal paternal uncertainty, regulations prohibit single women from using ARTs. As the *Book* argues, "it is unfair on men if single women are allowed to use donated sperm and conceive children because only women can have their own children" (Yu et al., 2015, p.42). This explains the disparity in reproductive rights mentioned in Chapter 1, such as the permission for single men to freeze sperm while denying single women the option to freeze eggs. When men fertilize eggs with their own sperm, paternity is confirmed. Conversely, when women employ ARTs and potentially become single mothers, the institution of marriage and the consent of a husband are absent, leaving paternity unconfirmed. However, this rationale of fairness reflects a deeply patriarchal stance toward single mothers, prioritizing male interests.

Not only do ARTs regulations, but also population policies, strictly situate childbirth in the sphere of heterosexual marriage. The thirteenth clause of the Regulations on ARTs stipulates that "clinics cannot perform ARTs on couples or single women who cannot conceive children according to population policies." According to article seventeen of the Population and Family Planning Law (*ren kou yu ji hua sheng yu fa*), for example, "citizens have the right to conceive children, but they are also obliged to follow family planning policies. Both husbands and wives are responsible for family planning." The policies grant individuals reproductive rights but only allow married heterosexual couples to conceive children. As legal scholar Guanyang Dong(2008) points out, reproductive rights remain the domain of legally married couples rather than extending to all citizens. Another legal scholar, Yu Feng (2016), concurs that only married individuals can legitimately exercise reproductive rights.

The son of no one

Chinese policymakers have restricted single women's access to ARTs to avoid single motherhood in order to mitigate the potential ambiguities surrounding legal paternity. Such paternal uncertainty is unique because no real men act as legal fathers. I borrow Nancy Dowd's term "the son of no one" (1997, p.40) here to describe the children raised by single mothers because these children lack legal paternal recognition.[4] In cases of divorce or death, children typically retain a link to their fathers, but in single motherhood via ARTs, the legal father's identity remains elusive.

As I mentioned in Chapter 2, the open-up of Chinese society has ushered in liberal attitudes toward marriage and family. Ideas of freedom suffuse ARTs, which "liberalize" the biological limits to kinship and make new types of families possible. As Franklin puts it:

> A pattern of flexible adjustment to both traditional kinship norms (however these may be defined) and the creation of alternative kinship possibilities, including new scientific options for parenthood, have characterized the transformation of kinship in the early twenty-first century. (2013, p.1.)

Indeed, ARTs challenge traditional notions of procreative sexuality and the association between genetics and marital bonds (Edwards, 2004). The legal mother may not necessarily be the biological mother, and the legal and biological fathers need not be the same individual. With the help of ARTs, new family forms such as single motherhood and homosexual families become possible.

Policymakers grappling with legal paternal uncertainty reflect on emerging family structures, such as single motherhood. They perceive single motherhood as a concern, emphasizing the pivotal role of fathers in child-rearing. As exemplified in the case "The Legal Status of the Children who are Born from Artificial Insemination after Couples Divorce," the Supreme Court prioritized establishing legal paternity before ruling on the financial obligations of the father toward his daughter. The *Book* explains how women's lives will change if they raise children alone: "Single mothers will shoulder the

---

[4] Nancy Dowd (1997) adopted the term from the New Jersey Supreme Court case Gubernat v. Deremer (1995). Under English Common Law, a child without a known father was often referred to as "the son of no one" and typically did not bear a surname. However, the Supreme Court in Gubernat v. Deremer rejected this English tradition, instead advocating for the protection of the child's interests by allowing them to assume the father's surname automatically.

burden of both housework and making money. Not only will her children's lives be changed, but their own life will be influenced" (Yu et al., 2015, p.41). The *Book* underscores the value of fatherhood in alleviating mothers from the tension between professional careers and family responsibilities. Tracy, a professional in the financial sector whom I encountered at a feminist gathering, epitomizes this dilemma. While intrigued by topics such as single women's access to ARTs and reproductive rights, she opposed the idea of single motherhood. Tracy's stance stemmed from her personal experience navigating the challenges of the workplace:

> When a colleague becomes pregnant, there is an implicit assumption that she won't be as productive as before. She will encounter huge discrimination. . … It is common for women to quit their jobs after marriage. Marriage is a protection for them (Tracy, 2016).

Tracy perceived the workplace as hostile toward working mothers, implying that they must exert greater effort than their male counterparts and perhaps forego motherhood to thrive professionally. The alternative, she suggested, is for women to retreat to domestic roles, allowing husbands to assume the primary breadwinner role. Tracy's narrative underscores the gendered division of labor and the obstacles confronting career-oriented women, consistent with existing research highlighting barriers to women's career advancement (Mate, McDonald, and Do, 2019; Coleman, 2019). She implied that single women encounter similar hurdles in navigating these challenges, let alone single mothers juggling both work and family pressures.

Will lesbian households face similar societal pressure? According to the *Book*, financial difficulty applies to lesbian couples even though their households are headed by two people. The *Book* introduces a case in the U.S,

> A lesbian couple were artificially inseminated with donated sperm. One woman gave birth to a baby, and the other gave birth to twins. One woman went out for work, and the other stayed home to care for the three children. After the couple broke up, the working mother initially agreed to pay the stay-at-home mum a $1,000 monthly fee for living expenses, but she later refused due to financial hardship (Yu et al., 2015, p.73).

This case underscores the *Book*'s argument regarding the significance of the division of labor based on sex rather than gender roles. Even though one lesbian mother assumed the breadwinner role traditionally held by a father, she was unable to single-handedly sustain the family's needs as a biological father might.

While some interviewees rationalize the challenges of single motherhood by emphasizing the father's role in child-rearing, this explanation proves problematic for Official Q, who worked in a local family planning department and saw herself as a feminist official. I interviewed her not only for her expertise in family planning policies but also because she intended to freeze her eggs. She expressed her reluctance towards marriage, citing the strain she witnessed in her sister's marital life. Official Q (2017) depicted her sister-in-law as "a typical Chinese husband." He provided material support while leaving the bulk of child-rearing responsibilities to her sister. Despite her sister's efforts in managing daily routines and overseeing their children's education, her sister-in-law remained disengaged, indulging in video games after work without contributing to parenting duties. Official Q lamented the cultural acceptance of men's minimal involvement in childcare, contrasting it sharply with the disproportionate burden placed on women. According to her, societal expectations hold women accountable for all aspects of child-rearing, from their dietary habits to their future prospects in marriage and employment.

The belief that women need husbands to effectively raise children not only simplifies the dual burden of work and family for women but also perpetuates discrimination against them in the workplace. However, if we question this rationale for child-rearing, what other factors contribute to the fear surrounding single motherhood over single fatherhood in contemporary society? In trying to answer this question, I interviewed single mothers who used ARTs to conceive children. Through their interactions with officials at local family planning departments, they could explain how the state is so invested in shoring up the traditional division of labor and heterosexual marriage. In addition, I wanted to understand how policymakers deal with the absence of legal paternity. Accordingly, I asked the single mothers how they negotiated restrictions on single motherhood.

The officials in my study viewed the absence of fatherhood as a social outlier. For them, single motherhood falls outside patriarchal control. They maintained both mothers and fathers are necessary for properly structured families. Consider a passage in the *Book* that defines families with single mothers as "incomplete:" "in contemporary society, single mothers and children born from 'incomplete' families are discriminated against" (Yu et al., 2015, p.41). This passage corresponds with the tradition of patrilineal kinship in China. In ancient Chinese society, social relations were based on bloodline. "There were five basic relationships for humans:father-son, sovereign-subject, husband-wife, elder brother-younger brother, friend-friend" (Huang and Gove, 2012, p.11). The father-son relationship held paramount importance, with social recognition contingent upon it. A child born to a man's legally married wife would be considered his proper heir (*di zi*) and thus inherit all of his estates and titles upon his death. A son born to a woman who was not married to the father would be considered a bastard (*si sheng zi*). Accordingly, he would not enjoy the same rights as the proper heir. Indeed, prior to the enactment of the Marriage Law in 1950, children born out of wedlock were not afforded the same privileges as children of legitimate birth.

The repackaging of traditional Confucian patrilineal lineage in contemporary society represents a reversal, showcasing the process of spiral modernization. In contemporary Chinese society, what holds more significance for a child is not merely financial stability but rather social acknowledgment. Through this study, I discovered that officials regarded the fertilization of women outside of heterosexual marriage as deviant and socially unacceptable. They perceived marriage as a privileged institution for both conceiving and nurturing children, believing that the involvement of both parents, particularly fathers, conferred social identities upon offspring. Families without fathers do not fit the norm and will, therefore, encounter social discrimination. Weiwei's experience exemplifies this perspective. She conceived a son with donated sperm in the United States. In filling in the household registration form, Weiwei explained to the local family planning department official that she would have to leave the section on her child's father blank because she did not know the father. The official then gave her a disdainful look and asked, "Why did you have sex with him if you did not know him very well? How come you could not remember where you had sex with him?" (Weiwei, 2017). The official's disdainful reaction implied a condemnation of Weiwei's perceived irresponsibility and moral character for conceiving a child outside of wedlock.

As the major role of fathers is to provide children with social identities, their function is symbolic. Xiao Wang's interactions with public hospital workers and state officials illustrate the symbolic function that fathers perform in Chinese society. According to Xiao Wang, although officials do not count on fathers to raise children, they are concerned about the blankness left by paternal absence. Xiao Wang was homosexual. When she accepted my interview, she had already conceived children, having injected the sperm of her girlfriend's cousin. "Single women need to overcome challenges when they conceive children," Xiao Wang (2017) said. Before a domestic hospital allowed her to deliver her child, she needed to provide information about the child's father. Doctors and nurses then pushed her to make up fathers' names. Later, when she registered the child to her household, officials also asked her to make up a name. Both the doctors and officials did not care about the identity of the child's biological father. Neither did they consider the fact that making up a fictional father would have left Xiao Wang to shoulder all of the responsibility for childcare. As Xiao Wang (2017) said, "They just needed a name with which to fill in the blanks."

In addition to filling in the blanks of household registration forms, to reinforce traditions of lineage and societal norms, officials erect other barriers for single mothers, such as children's restricted access to public schooling and healthcare. Lao Bai was a lesbian. She conceived a child using donated sperm in the United States. I knew her from the WeChat group run by the feminist salon that supported single mothers. Upon returning to China, Lao Bai contacted her local family planning department to register her child in her household. When it came to filling in the information concerning the child's parentage, Lao Bai (2017) recounted, "I told the staff there that I conceived a child but that the child's father was missing." The reason for this, she explained, was that "the staff would not understand sperm donation" (Lao Bai, 2017). Although she did not reveal that she had used donated sperm, the local officials were still concerned about the legal identity of the child's father. After Lao Bai repeatedly confirmed that her child's father was missing and would never show up, the officials allowed her to leave the information section on the father blank. Still, despite this successful household registration, the officials still warned that her child might encounter difficulties in the future. "You should be responsible for fines and other issues with household registration," they told her (Lao Bai, 2017). "Some hospitals need children's fathers to be present before treating them. If you buy insurance for children, some companies require the consent of their fathers. It is difficult for your child to live in this society without her father" (Lao Bai, 2017).

To "fill in the blanks," some single mothers organize "marriages of convenience" (*xing hun*), in which they marry known or unknown men as a means to construct nominal paternal identities and fulfill the social preference for "complete" families.

According to her ethnography in China, Wang (2019) found homosexual people cope with the heteronormative family model through cooperative marriages. As Ingraham (2011) states, marriage "is a rite of passage for appropriate heterosexual identity and membership" (p.307). Nominal fathers, though lacking biological ties to their children, hold symbolic significance, with symbolic fatherhood outweighing actual kinship. This concept parallels Nancy A. Naples's notion of doing family (2001), wherein family relations are constructed to conform to social norms rather than develop genuine personal connections. Marriages of convenience do not aim to nurture relationships between children and fathers but rather to fulfill normative family structures by orchestrating weddings and securing nominal fathers. It is noteworthy that while men pursue genetic paternity, women seek symbolic paternity to navigate societal and state expectations.

Xiao Wang and Weiwei's experiences provide illustrative examples. Xiao Wang considered a marriage of convenience before eventually deciding to leave the section on her child's fatherhood blank. She tried to find a gay man on Douban who could act as her child's legal father on a birth permission certificate and household registration form, although ultimately, she gave up the idea.[5] However, she proceeded to orchestrate a lavish wedding ceremony with another man, selected for his societal conformity and acceptance by relatives rather than his involvement in childcare or financial support. She (2017) described the process in the following way:

> One man was qualified. He worked in the financial industry. He was handsome as well. He was the man that relatives would be satisfied with. … He did not need to pay the costs of childbirth. All we needed to do was host a grand wedding ceremony. For me, the ceremony was like an explanation. We declared to our friends and relatives that we were normal. Then these people would never bother us again.

The fake bridegroom she chose matched her relatives' criteria for a qualified, handsome, and well-paid husband. For Xiao Wang, the ceremony served as a facade, signaling normality to friends and family and deflecting further scrutiny.

Weiwei initially considered fabricating a husband or a fictional father for her son to facilitate household registration. However, she abandoned these ideas upon realizing the potential consequences for her child's future prospects, including educational, property, and marital considerations. She (2017) had once seen a notice from her local police station, saying that "if divorced families need to change children's names, children's legal mothers and fathers should both sign the forms and agree." Despite the short-term ease these solutions might offer, the long-term implications, such as the inability of a fictional father to sign legal documents, outweighed their benefits. Nevertheless, she still invited one of her friends to be her son's nominal father. They hosted a grand ceremony in her village, and many of her relatives witnessed it. After this, her relatives no longer questioned the fact that her son did not have a father. Marriages of convenience or finding nominal fathers for children allow single mothers to observe filial piety and satisfy their relatives. These constructions of fatherhood serve to confer a normal social status onto single mothers and their children.

---

[5] Douban is a Chinese social networking website, which allows users to create and share content associated with food, films, books, music, and activities.

Summary

This chapter delved deep into the intricate dynamics surrounding virginity and single motherhood and explains why Chinese regulations specify marriage as a precondition for women's use of ARTs. Prohibiting ARTs among single women recapitulates the prescription that marriage is necessary for both biological and legal paternity. On the one hand, the clinicians I interviewed equated single women with virgin women, positing that ARTs could compromise their hymen and virginity. According to their perspective, a woman's loss of virginity prior to marriage might provoke doubts about her fidelity in her future husband's mind, potentially casting uncertainty on the lineage of their offspring. Consequently, restricting single women's access to ARTs is viewed as a mate-guarding strategy. This chapter illustrates how interviewees emphasized this traditional evolutionary belief in paternal uncertainty to counterbalance liberal sexual attitudes prevailing in China.

On the other hand, policymakers and clinicians justified the ban on single women's use of ARTs by citing concerns over single motherhood, which inherently lacks legal paternity. By emphasizing the significance of legal paternity, officials aimed not to ensure paternal commitment to parenting but rather to denounce the practice of fertilizing unmarried women as deviant and socially unacceptable. In essence, they sought merely a man's presence to conform to heteronormative cultural norms. This emphasis on legal paternity finds its roots in Confucian principles of patrilineal families, as officials revisited this traditional notion to grapple with the challenges posed by emerging family structures, such as single motherhood.

This chapter uncovered another facet of spiral modernization through the reflections of my interviewees on liberal attitudes toward premarital sex and single motherhood. These reflections lead to policy reversals concerning traditional notions of paternal uncertainty, whether rooted in evolutionary psychology or Confucian patrilineal beliefs. The next chapter will address controversial fertility treatment regulations on patient management. It will show how my interviewees viewed clinicians and officials as sources of uncertainty, with this distrust reflecting broader social conflicts in China.

Chapter 5

A crisis of trust

Over the past decades, our society has undergone unprecedented changes......Reform and development can continue only when society is stable (*san shi duo nian lai, wo guo she hui fa sheng de bian ge qian suo wei you.....zhe chong fen zheng ming, zhi you she hui wen ding, gai ge fa zhan can neng bu duan tui jin*).
—Chairman Xi Jinping

Negligent treatment

I opened this book with a medical dispute outside P Clinic. The couple's complaint was not resolved. I was told by Dr. D a few months after my fieldwork that they still protested outside P Clinic. Their ongoing protests underscored the profound uncertainty woven into the fabric of the fertility journey, a theme explored in Chapter 3. No clinic can guarantee pregnancy or rule out fetal deformity, a reality acknowledged by regulatory frameworks emphasizing meticulous patient care. *The Book* explains,

> Due to many factors resulting in infertility, the diagnosis and treatment process of infertility is complicated, and the treatment cycle is long. Therefore, we require high standards for the quality of clinical service. Clinicians should understand the process of diagnosis and treatment and patient management (Yu et al., 2015, p.268).

Fertility treatment can be a stressful and anxious experience for many people going through it, thus requiring a high standard of care and practice.

However, amid this complexity, I encountered patients like Yuetian, whose uncertainty stemmed not solely from treatment outcomes but also from skepticism toward their chosen clinics. Yuetian received IVF treatment at P Clinic. She (2016) believed that clinics only recommend expensive treatments so as to make more money,

> Clinicians recommended Western medicine. They said that Western medicine was purer than domestic medicine. However, I've heard from other patients that some women chose not to use Western medicine so as to avoid miscarriages because it was hard to control the dosage. An

overdose could easily cause a miscarriage. I do not know whether I will get pregnant. Perhaps the clinic needs to make money. Hopefully, Western medicine might work eventually.

Yuetian's uncertainty about her pregnancy did not solely stem from medical risks inherent to IVF but rather from a pervasive distrust in the clinic's intentions. She feared that profit-driven motives might influence treatment decisions, potentially compromising her chances of conceiving.

Yuetian's skepticism towards medical treatment was not unique; it echoed a broader sentiment of distrust in China's healthcare system, where the pursuit of profit often overshadowed patient welfare. Throughout my fieldwork, I encountered individuals deeply wary of the motives driving medical practitioners, perceiving them as solely motivated by financial gain. For example, when patients queued up to register with clinicians outside P Clinic, they often talked about which clinicians were best and compared notes on the costs of their various treatment plans. They wanted to make sure that the cost was reasonable. If they paid more than other patients, they began to question the integrity of their clinicians. One day, a woman scolded her clinician after learning that another woman had been charged only 10% of what she had paid for the "same" treatment. From that moment on, the woman regarded her clinician as unreliable, believing that clinicians tended to recommend expensive treatments.

This erosion of trust can be traced back to the privatization of healthcare in China, a transformation detailed in Chapter 2. As state investment dwindled during Deng's era, healthcare became increasingly privatized, placing the burden of financial responsibility squarely on patients. Rachel Leow's (2014) analysis aptly characterizes this shift as a transition towards an out-of-pocket healthcare model, where rising costs exacerbate public distrust.

Yuetian's distrust deepened when a community clinic once refused to help her in an emergency. The clinic's staff explained that she should seek medical attention from the clinic that had initially provided her with reproductive treatment. Yuetian did not buy this. "We used to call doctors 'angels in white,'" Yuetian (2016) told me, "but now they are only interested in making money. They are so indifferent that they did not help me in an emergency." Yuetian's experience illustrates that doctors in China are often praised not just for their excellent medical skills but also for their philanthropic and selfless attitude. Norman Bethune, for example, is held up as a role model of medical altruism. In his essay "In Memory of Norman Bethune," Chairman Mao wrote: "Comrade Bethune's spirit, his utter devotion to others without any thought of himself, was shown in his great sense of responsibility in his work and his great warmheartedness towards all comrades and the people" (1939, p.337). Mao's eulogy for Bethune extolled not just his medical prowess but also his unwavering commitment to serving others, a standard by which doctors in China were once revered. The discrepancy between this idealized view and the reality of market-driven medicine undermines the moral authority of doctors. Yuetian's invocation of "angels in white" (*bai yi tian shi*) encapsulates this dissonance, emphasizing the moral imperative of medical practice. When doctors prioritize profit over patient care, they forfeit this moral legitimacy, eroding trust and perpetuating a cycle of skepticism and distrust. Thus, while the community clinic's actions may have been ostensibly reasonable, they violated Yuetian's deeply held expectations and further undermined her trust in the medical system.

Alongside concerns about profit-driven clinics, the patients in this study also complained about the lack of personalized care from clinicians. Hence, they were not sure whether their treatment plans were effective. The patients' complaints reflect the imbalances within China's medical resources, a legacy of the dismantling of the three-tier medical system during Deng's era. As resources became increasingly concentrated in top-tier public clinics in urban areas, patients tended to crow into these clinics. With the number of patients increasing, it is difficult to make an appointment with doctors, especially top specialists in highly reputable hospitals. The demand for appointments creates business opportunities for appointment touts (*hao fan zi*), who peddle slots with top doctors for extortionate prices. Patients are willing to pay for these slots to avoid waiting for weeks or months for an appointment.

At P Clinic, a prominent public fertility center, the demand for appointments reached staggering levels, spawning a lucrative market for appointment touts who exploit patients' desperation. To combat this, the clinic implemented stringent registration protocols, requiring in-person registration with a litany of documentation. This resulted in long queues forming outside the clinic well before opening hours, with patients anxiously vying for appointment slots on a "first come, first served" basis. On the first day of my fieldwork, I went to the clinic at 8 a.m. (the clinic opened an hour later). When I arrived, I was surprised to see that the queue outside of the clinic was already more than 100 meters long. In fact, I found that many patients had been queuing in front of the clinic since before 6 a.m. in the hope of successfully registering with a clinician.

Even after securing appointments, patients faced further hurdles, contending with lengthy pre-consultation procedures exacerbated by the sheer volume of patients. These included paying, undergoing a medical examination, and checking their certificates. Due to the large number of patients in the clinic, every task required queuing. "There are too many people waiting in the clinic," a patient (source anonymized, 2016c) complained. "I need to stay in the clinic for one day. I have taken so many days off this month in order to meet clinicians and conduct medical checks. My boss is unsatisfied with my work" (source anonymized, 2016c). I noticed people often jumped in queues. The information desk was surrounded by many patients and their families, all asking different questions at once. Assistants did not know which question to answer first.

Consultation rooms were also full of people. Although Dr. D's consultation sessions started at 11 a.m. every morning, patients were waiting outside her consultation room from 10 a.m. Some of them were anxious and kept asking Dr. D's assistant whether they could enter. Patients had to queue outside until they were called in. However, some of them rushed in to meet Dr. D without being called. They could not help but enter the consultation room to ask questions. Dr. D, like many clinicians, grappled with the challenge of maintaining order amid the frenzy, often forced to juggle multiple consultations simultaneously. Her assistant kept asking patients who had come into the consultation room to wait outside. Although some patients obliged, the room was soon full again.

Having spent a long time and a lot of money registering with doctors, patients have high expectations of doctors and demand longer consultations. Nevertheless, clinicians have to treat patients very quickly if they are to meet all of those who have registered. Long hours and high workloads among doctors often mean that they allocate only short time slots to treating individual patients. Indeed, Dr. D needed to treat around 50 patients in just two hours of consultation. She glanced through patients' medical records and came up with treatment plans.

The lack of consultation time left patients questioning the individualization of their treatment plans. Accordingly, they did not trust clinicians' advice and felt uncertain about treatment outcomes. For instance, Zixuan (2016), a 27-year-old seeking IVF treatment at P Clinic, lamented the missed opportunities for early intervention in preserving her fertility:

> I've been married for five years. In order to have children as soon as possible, we used test papers every time before we had sex. However, I did not get pregnant even though we always had sex during my ovulatory period. I started consulting clinicians here three years ago. Every time I met a clinician, she said I was too young to use IVF. They also did not allow me to try egg freezing. She encouraged me to have sex outside of my ovulatory period, too. I tried with my husband for a while, and I still did not get pregnant. At this stage, I was finally able to conduct the six hormones test. I found I no longer produce eggs. I do not have eggs to use (*ran bing luan*). Do not merely adopt clinicians' advice. They are not reliable.

Despite her proactive efforts to seek medical guidance, she felt let down by clinicians who dismissed her concerns based on age rather than conducting thorough evaluations. She felt that the clinicians had misinformed her and consequently no longer trusted their decisions. This time, Zixuan said that she would insist on fertility treatment no matter what the clinicians suggested.

Caifeng, who was 40 years old, had a similar experience to that of Zixuan. She went to P Clinic for a consultation about egg freezing. She had been to several hospitals, but none were willing to provide the service. I interviewed her after she had finished her consultation with a clinician at P Clinic. She (2016) was disappointed about the appointment, saying, "The clinician with whom I registered today met me for only five minutes. She did not fully understand my situation. Even if she recommended fertility treatment, I doubt its outcomes." For Caifeng, the clinician's conclusions seemed arbitrary and problematic, for she had not grasped Caifeng's situation—understandably, given that the consolation had lasted just five minutes. "I plan to register with an expert for a later consultation on the technology," said Caifeng (2016).

Fertility treatments can be fraught with anxiety, fear, and often unrealistic expectations. Patients demand psychological and emotional support in addition to technical help. I met Lang in the feminist salon. She conceived a baby in the United States. She (2016) recounted her experience at an American hospital, where the considerate care she received alleviated her anxieties:

> Delivering a child in the United States was less painful than even menstruation. The hospital prepared all the other things, including my food, sanitary products, milk, napkins, etc. In order to help me sleep after labor, nurses took care of my children at night. They listed my daily tasks on a blackboard in my room, such as sit-up exercises. These exercises aimed at eliminating my pain rather than just relieving it. Nurses emphasized again and again that I could take pills if I felt pain. I was also impressed that nurses in US hospitals can remember everyone's name. Some of their staff only saw my babies once, but they remembered their names. When I left the hospital, every member of staff congratulated me.

Lang did not praise US doctors' and nurses' excellent medical skills or superior knowledge. Instead, it was the considerate service that she received at the US clinic that relieved her anxieties. The clinic was willing to spend time listening to patients and forging relationships of trust with them. It tried to deliver a less painful experience by taking measures such as preparing maternal necessities, reminding Lang of pain-relieving exercises, and remembering her name. In sharp contrast, Lang regarded the Chinese medical system as much less considerate. She complained that Chinese doctors were unwilling to spend time satisfying patients' extra needs. "In domestic fertility clinics," she (2016) said, "doctors take women's pain for granted." She blamed Chinese doctors for not giving women pain relief medicines since prescribing painkillers is not mandatory. Apathy dented clinicians' professionalism, she claimed.

During my observations at P Clinic, I found that patients often turned to other patients for help when they did not receive support from clinicians. They told me that they had formed support groups both online and offline. Paul Rabinow has termed these support groups "biosociality" (1996). The concept focuses on how patients with similar diagnoses form connections based on shared experiences and mutual support. On one hand, biosociality provides patients with emotional support. Patients at P Clinic had a variety of socio-economic backgrounds and were from all parts of China. For married women, their husbands usually accompanied them for the initial consultations. For other scheduled visits, they often visited the clinic alone. If patients did not already reside in Beijing, they had to find accommodation in the city for one or two months.[1] I found many patients rented apartments together. Despite the small living space, one patient said that living with other patients conjured up a sense of community. On the other hand, biosociality provided valuable information-sharing platforms, enabling patients to navigate complex treatment decisions. For example, patients told me that they organized WeChat discussion groups so as to compare treatment plans.

Patients' eagerness to form biosociality reflects their distrust of clinics. As I observed at P Clinic, expensive medical care, tedious administrative processes, limited medical resources in remote areas, and poor service all result in patients being dissatisfied with doctors. However, dialogues among patients often aggravated their uncertainty about treatment plans. In P Clinic's waiting lounge, one patient complained that her clinician "said that she could no

---

[1] The limited availability of medical resources in remote areas forces patients to visit doctors in urban areas (Vedom and Cao, 2011). The nearest hotel to P Clinic charged patients ¥100 per night. Given that most patients could not afford to stay in the hotel, they rented apartments nearby. A two-bed apartment could host at least six tenants, each paying ¥30–50 per night. Saving money was important to patients pursuing fertility treatment. China's healthcare insurance system does not cover infertility treatment until the National Healthcare Security Administration proposed the medical insurance fund to cover ARTs in order to ease the financial burden of infertility treatment on families in 2023, which can cost several thousands of RMB. After the National Healthcare Security Administration announced the proposal, Beijing, China's capital, was the first city to extend medical insurance coverage to a slew of fertility services including IUI, embryo transfer and sperm selection.

longer explain things to me. I can only follow her instructions"(source anonymized, 2016d). She then asked another patient to check her medicine list. The woman replied, "I took this medicine before, but it was ineffective. There was another brand, which was also Western. My clinician recommended this brand" (source anonymized, 2016e). Another woman joined their conversation and shared her views: "There are only two or three kinds of ovulation stimulation drugs," she said (source anonymized, 2016f). "I mix and inject them together. However, my clinician said that different patients should inject differently according to their sensitivity to drugs"(source anonymized, 2016f). The patient told me she ended up more confused than when she had first asked for help.

Clinicians often discouraged the idea of biosociality, asserting their authority over treatment decisions. Dr. L told a story about a woman who insisted on freezing eggs. Since she no longer produced eggs, Dr. L told her that pursuing egg freezing would be a waste of money. The woman, however, did not believe Dr. L, who she thought was tricking her. Dr. L claimed that tall tales about egg freezing falsely undermined clinicians' authority. She did not understand why the public trusted celebrities such as Jinglei Xu, who had no background in embryology, over clinicians who had been treating infertility for years.

During my fieldwork, I also noticed that patients were eager to get involved in the process of medical decision-making by asking for detailed explanations about their condition, taking their medical records home, taking photos of their records, or making audio recordings of consultations. The eagerness to participate in medical decision-making also reflects patients' distrust of the medical plans made by clinicians. Nevertheless, clinicians do not support patients' involvement. Once, Dr. D got very angry when a woman tried to take photographs of her medical records. "Do not take photos!" she (2016d) snapped. "You do not understand this information. Everyone's treatment is different. And different clinicians might treat the same situation differently. There is no need to compare" (Dr. D, 2016d). Dr. D emphasized her authority in deciding treatment plans and downplayed patients' desire and ability to cope with medical information. Her reluctance to accommodate patient participation reflects a broader tension between patients' desire for autonomy and clinicians' insistence on professional authority. The disconnect between patients' expectations and clinicians' attitudes underscores the need for a more collaborative approach to healthcare, one that prioritizes patient-centered care and acknowledges patients as active partners in their treatment journey. Despite clinicians' reservations, patients' desire for involvement reflects a fundamental shift in healthcare dynamics, one that requires greater openness, communication, and mutual respect between patients and providers.

Inaction

In medical disputes, clinicians often bear the brunt of blame, but other stakeholders also come under scrutiny. For example, the couple outside P Clinic also blamed government officials for neglecting their situation, even though officials had no connection with their son's illness. Even in cases that did not develop into disputes eventually, similar grievances surfaced during my interviews with feminists who advocated for single women's reproductive autonomy, and single mothers navigated bureaucratic hurdles to register their children.

One such advocate I knew was Koby, a fellow member of a WeChat group focusing on single women's reproductive rights. She founded a non-government organization that lobbied for the liberalization of single women's access to ARTs. Despite China's significant population policy shifts from the One-Child Policy to the Three Children Policy, ARTs regulations have remained stagnant since 2003. Koby's frustration peaked when her proposal to the NPC in 2015 received a tepid response. The NPC responded that different levels of their organization needed to consider her proposal. Koby then waited for half a year, but a reply was still not forthcoming. "The People's Congress is too bureaucratic (*guan liao*) to take action," Koby (2017) complained.

As I discussed in Chapter 2, the decentralization of party power during Deng's era fostered flexibility and incentives for local officials. While this political reform spurred economic development, it also bred administrative inertia and an overreliance on superior officials' orders. This bureaucratic gridlock, termed "*guan liao*" by Koby, symbolized to her the stifling effect of entrenched hierarchies on proactive action.

The inertia of government officials can foster feelings of uncertainty among citizens regarding the efficacy of governmental processes. Sharing her experience with the Chinese Embassy, Lang complained about how officials were indifferent to her case. Lang and her girlfriend married in Las Vegas. She conducted IVF to give birth to a baby in the U.S. Although she could have conceived her children in China, she chose to conceive children in the U.S. in order to take up her children's right to US citizenship. To bring her babies to China, she needed to apply for travel certificates.[2] However, the Chinese Embassy declined her application, asking her to change the information on the babies' birth certificates because homosexual marriage is illegal in China. She asked the officials whether they would reconsider her application since it is

---

[2] Travel certificates are for children who are born in the United States but whose parents are Chinese.

difficult to change information on birth certificates issued in the United States.[3] Then, the official from the Chinese Embassy asked Lang to wait for an answer from his superior. After a few months of waiting, there was still no answer. "At that time," Lang (2016) told me, "I felt so angry about my identity as Chinese. Chinese officials did not put themselves in people's shoes."

Despite the complexities of US administrative procedures for altering birth certificates, Lang's ire was directed towards Chinese officials who offered little assistance and provided vague responses. Their indecision left her in limbo, unsure whether her application would ultimately be approved. The lack of clear communication and prolonged waiting periods exacerbated Lang's frustration, leading her to question her identity as a Chinese citizen and the reliability of governmental institutions. According to Lang (2016), "They did not simply say no. They asked me to wait and gave me indefinite answers. Therefore, I do not know if they will approve or not."

Lang's eventual resolution of the issue through legal channels in the US underscored the contrast between proactive action and bureaucratic inertia. Moreover, her subsequent encounter with her local neighborhood committee in Chaoyang District, Beijing, further eroded her trust in governmental entities. After returning to China, she received a call from her local neighborhood committee in Chaoyang District, Beijing, whose staff said that they had recently launched a survey about women of childbearing age. "You do not have the authority to obtain my information," Lang told them and hung up the phone. Lang's perception of the survey as a veiled attempt at surveillance rather than genuine outreach epitomized the erosion of trust stemming from governmental inaction and indifference.

Trust is built up not only based on individuals' past experiences but also on anticipated futures. People trust a government when they are confident that it will do what is right and fair. Even if that government is doing the right thing, people will lose faith in it if they do not believe that it is behaving properly. It is much easier to destroy trust than to build it. Once individuals lose trust, governments cannot simply restore it again. Regardless of whether the Chaoyang Neighborhood Committee's survey was genuine, Lang had no faith in its legitimacy. Her distrust of government serves as a cautionary tale, highlighting the fragility of trust in the face of bureaucratic inefficiency and indifference.

---

[3] Lang needed to appeal to a local court to obtain a court order. The court declined her appeal on the grounds that homosexual marriage was legal in the United States and hence there was no need to change the information.

People also complain about the ambiguity of the orders passed down from the CCP or their superiors, leading to uncertainty about the fulfillment of their requests. National regulations often lack specificity, resulting in varying interpretations among local officials. This ambiguity diminishes officials' motivation to enact policy changes. According to Koby (2017):

> Actually, many officials do not know how to take action. The national policies just mentioned that single women could not use ARTs. And local-level governments issue different policies. Jilin Province, for example, allows single women to use ARTs if they decide not to marry. The policy-making on single motherhood was quite chaotic.

Koby attributed the government's inaction on her request to revise ARTs regulations to the ambiguity surrounding policy interpretation and implementation. This inaction erodes public trust in local officials' ability to represent their interests. Even when officials adhere to national policies, they often bear the brunt of citizen anger as they operate at the frontline of policy implementation. Despite understanding the policy-making process, Koby doubted that government officials would safeguard single women's rights due to their indifference to her proposal to liberalize ARTs.

During a conversation at a feminist salon, I met Juzi, a journalist who had interviewed several officials about potential policy changes regarding single women's access to ARTs. Juzi discovered conflicting opinions among officials, with some vehemently opposing single women's access to ARTs, citing family planning policies, while others emphasized the importance of protecting single women's reproductive rights, also referencing family planning policies. "The stance of family planning policies towards single women remains uncertain," Juzi (2017) admitted.

In illustrating how policy ambiguity leads to uncertainty, I highlight the challenges faced by women attempting to conceive children without marriage certificates. In the previous chapter, I described the difficulty in registering children as household members in the absence of paternity information. Many local officials did not allow them to leave their father's information blank. However, some single women did manage to negotiate with officials. Here, I present examples of women who successfully navigated these policy restrictions, though they all concur that the journey was still fraught with uncertainty. First, upon pregnancy, single women must obtain birth permission certificates (*zhun sheng zheng*) from local family planning commissions before they can give birth in public hospitals. While some provinces, like Hubei and Sichuan since 2013, have streamlined the process for single women to obtain these certificates, others leave it to local officials' discretion.[4] Zhang Wen, whom I met through a feminist salon, underwent sperm donation in the United States and gave birth to a girl in a private hospital in Beijing in 2016. She felt frustrated when she dealt with officials in a local family planning commission in her street neighborhood (*jie dao*). Despite Beijing's relaxed family planning policies during her pregnancy, ambiguity persisted at the local level regarding single mothers' eligibility for birth planning certificates. Thus, officials hesitated to grant her a certificate. "All they said was 'we cannot decide. We need to ask the superior official.'," said Zhang Wen (2017). Not knowing whether she would obtain a certificate, Zhang Wen chose to give birth in a private hospital.

Second, once they have successfully given birth, single mothers reach the final step in their long journey toward reproduction: household registration. Household records (*hu kou*) encompass an individual's name, date of birth, education, marital status, and residency status. Failure to register children in a household will result in their being denied access to public education and healthcare. Single mothers must pay social maintenance fees before registering their children, a practice introduced post-implementation of family planning policies. Initially termed "extra birth fees" in the 1980s and later renamed "unplanned birth fines" in 1994, these charges were formalized as "social maintenance fees" in the 2001 Population and Family Planning Law. According to Article 41, "Citizens who give birth to babies that do not comply with Article 18 of this law shall pay a social maintenance fee prescribed by law" (People's Congress, 2001). Violation of family planning policies includes conceiving children outside of heterosexual marriage and conceiving more than the number of children designated by family planning policies. As the Population and Family Planning Law notes, social maintenance fees are not fines. They are "economic compensation paid to society, as new births take up a lot of public and social resources" (People's Congress, 2001).

However, there is no specific standard for charging social maintenance fees, which makes people uncertain how much they should pay in order to

---

[4] Hubei Province was the first province to guarantee single women's right to a birth permission certificate, unlike other provinces, which left the matter to officials' discretion (Branigan, 2014). Accordingly, in Hubei Province, marriage certificates are no longer be required to obtain birth permission certificates. In Hubei Province, in cases of single parents, babies born through ARTs, or pregnancies involving unknown fathers, the mother can write a signed explanation. That is sufficient to apply for a birth permission certificate. Local health authorities will need to check the authenticity of the materials before issuing certificates. The new guidelines in Hubei Province also stipulate that the officials responsible for issuing birth permission certificates cannot set preconditions (such as that the applicant also request a marriage certificate) and they are not allowed to receive any fee in exchange for certificates.

successfully register households for their "illegal" children. According to the third clause of the Management Policies for Charging Social Maintenance Fees, "the standard by which social maintenance fees are charged depends on average annual income. Officials should also consider the income of applicants and the seriousness of the case when they decide the amount of payment" (The State Council of the People's Republic of China, 2002). This clause does not specify the amount of social maintenance fees. As a result, government policies in this area have been implemented in diverse ways, occasioning pervasive ambiguity. Local officials retain considerable influence in deciding payment amounts. They are then often criticized for abusing this power. For example, in Beijing, social maintenance fees range from 1 to 3 times household income, while in Liaoning Province, they can be as high as 5 to 10 times household income (Xinhua, 2017). Cities such as Shanghai are increasingly open to alternative conceptions of the family and have abolished social maintenance fees. Some cities, however, still resist accepting single mothers and impose exorbitant fees. Miss Zhang (2017), who worked at C egg freezing agency, told me that clients from second and third-tier cities always complained about such regional policy differences:

> Officials in their cities never knew how to register single mothers' children in their households. Officials always replied that they needed to ask their superiors. And their superiors' answers were inconsistent. There was no standard answer regarding the social maintenance fees to be paid. Different local governments charged different social maintenance fees. Sometimes, local officials even took away low-income families' food and cows as punishment.

According to Miss Zhang, the most acute concern her clients faced was whether the government would legalize their children and how much money they would have to pay for the privilege. The amounts charged depend on how local officials interpret the law.

In addition to social maintenance fees stipulated in national laws, some local governments impose additional requirements for single mothers before their children are granted household registration. For instance, Beijing mandates paternal DNA tests; without them, children cannot be registered. In 2016, the central government issued How to Register the Accommodation of Those without Household Registration (*guo wu yuan ban gong ting guan yu jie jue wu hu kou ren yuan deng ji hu kou wen ti de yi jian*) to ease the process of requesting DNA tests. "Children who are born without state permission or who are born to unmarried parents," it states, "can register their accommodation using their father's or mothers' IDs and a written explanation of wedlock births. Single parents also need to present the results of maternity or paternity tests to prove that the children belong to them" (The State Council of the People's Republic of China, 2016). Despite this, due to the central government's ambiguous stance on single motherhood, lower-level officials often err on the side of caution, enforcing strict registration policies to avoid potential errors.

Weiwei recalled the cautious approach of local officials due to unclear guidance from the central government. "I contacted my local family planning department in a neighborhood committee," she (2017) recounted.

> The staff in the family planning department had never dealt with anything like this before. So as not to be blamed by her superiors, the member of staff reported my case to her superiors. After one month, an official there asked me to provide information including marital status, childbirth status, child status, father's information, etc. Then, the official's superiors reported my information to higher authorities. Approval from these higher authorities took another month to come in. After approval, a member of staff cleared me to receive a family planning certificate stamped by three tiers of government, including the neighborhood committee, a community committee, and the district government.

Given that national policies do not specify whether single women can register children in their households, officials relied on the judgment of their superiors to mitigate potential blame in case of adverse outcomes. Officials in different government departments were involved in the household registration process, according to Weiwei, evading responsibility and shifting the blame onto others.

For some of my informants, this regulatory ambiguity opened up room for negotiation around policies. As an old Chinese saying goes, "Although the government designs policies, people have their ways of getting around them" (*shang you zheng ce, xia you dui ce*). Building relationships (*gao guan xi*) is a common way in which my informants solved uncertain situations in China. Xiao Wang (2017), for example, said that the local government would not take action until you knew a member of their staff:

> The documents seemed to assure us that we could register our household and afford the fines, but I still contacted an official that my friend knew in advance. We sent him some gifts. This is China, you know. And everything is about *Guan Xi*.

Guan Xi, an indefinite concept that translates as "relations" in English, represents "an essential part of China's national character at any time or place" (Huang, 1987, p.959). Sociologist Xiaotong Fei has explained how the notion of *guan xi* emerged historically, comparing relations in traditional China with "ripples formed from a stone thrown in a lake, each circle spreading out from the center becomes more distant and at the same time more significant" (1992, p.65). It was seen as possible for everyone in the land to be related to everyone else. Relationships could be built through friendship, education, professional connections, similar origins, hobbies, etc. Xiao Wang established a connection with an official, having been introduced by her friend.

Moreover, *Guan Xi* signifies reciprocity. It is a mechanism of exchanging favors for indebtedness. The privatization of power during China's economic reform has significantly increased the incentives for officials to engage in corruption (Hao and Johnston, 2002). Officials abuse power for private gain. Xiao Wang provided vivid narrative depictions of the gift exchange system. Xiao Wang sent an official monetary gifts. In return, the official facilitated the process of registering her household. Miss Yang, a member of staff at O egg freezing agency, also described how a client from Wenzhou successfully negotiated her fines by sending official money. Since there was no standard for determining social maintenance fees and different districts in Wenzhou were charging different amounts, local officials could decide how much people should pay. The client bribed an official with ¥50,000 so as to reduce her social maintenance fees. The official accepted the money, allowing the client to pay reduced social maintenance fees in return.

It is an unspoken rule among Chinese officials that one has to build relationships. Doing so removes legal, moral, and cognitive barriers that hinder administrative processes through corrupt agreements. Even ostensibly rational and evidence-based policy-making underscores the importance of gifts in solidifying mutual aid and obligation relationships. Official H from the NHFPC illustrated the point by telling the story of Zexi Wei, which received enormous public attention during my fieldwork. Zexi Wei, a 20-year-old undergraduate, was diagnosed with synovial sarcoma in 2014. He searched for "cancer treatment hospital" on Baidu.com (a Chinese version of Google). The Second Hospital of the Beijing Armed Police Corps was ranked first in the Baidu search results. Wei Zexi chose the hospital and conducted dendritic cells-cytokine-induced killer cells (DC-CIK) immunotherapy treatment. Although he spent ¥200,000 on his treatment, it proved unsuccessful. He died in 2016. According to Official H, DC-CIK was an ineffective treatment and cannot address cancer. The reason that medical insurance agencies could list DC-CIK as a treatment for cancer was that "the researchers of DC-CIK maintained a good relationship with the MOH and Ministry of Social Insurance. They had some dinner parties and settled down the deal" (Official H,2017). Official H implied that officials did not thoroughly study the benefits and shortcomings of DC-CIK. According to her, sometimes officials' decisions are based on their relationship with the researchers, not evidence.

Guan Xi can assure people that they can achieve certain goals after exchanging gifts with officials, but it undermines the state's regulations, fairness, and integrity. As the Chinese political scientist Yi Liu argued, "the influence of corruption ... means that rules and regulations are losing their proper effect due to the destruction of procedure and institutionalization. ... The existence of corruption confuses social order ... social conflicts are inevitable" (2007, p.23). Speaking of the deterioration of the government's authority, Koby also referred to the case of Zexi Wei. She believed that the government failed to supervise biomedical products. "If clinics maintain good relationships with officials," she (2017) said, "they will allow clinics to sell any products as long as they can make money." According to Koby, the Chinese government's failure to establish effective and strong regulatory institutions to oversee healthcare stems from officials' corrupt practices. As a result, substandard medical products flood the market, damaging people's health.

Weapons of the weak

In the previous two sections, I described people who were uncertain about their treatment plans or solutions to their requests because they were unsatisfied with the medical and political system. The medical and political reform during Deng's era led to a few challenges, such as expensive healthcare, unbalanced medical resources, and officials' indifference to ordinary people's interests. The prevalent uncertainty observed during my research underscores people's lack of trust in formal institutions—whether pertaining to healthcare, the legal system, or local authorities. This study sheds light on the tensions existing between doctors and patients, as well as between officials and ordinary citizens, particularly concerning reproductive issues. For example, patients yearn for greater autonomy in treatment decisions, while doctors often assert their authority in a manner that dismisses patient concerns. Similarly, single mothers seek clearer guidance on registering children's households, while local officials exhibit sluggishness in addressing citizen requests. Over time, I came to understand why some single mothers adopt an "us-versus-them" discourse, viewing officials as antagonists.

Since fertility issues easily lead to disputes, ARTs, if managed unwell, will exercise a carnivalesque, subversive power that challenges the authority of clinics, officials, and governmental policies. Therefore, the national regulations require clinicians to maintain proper relationships with patients. As the *Book* argues, "with the development of medical public services, clinical medicine has developed from a one-to-one relationship between doctors and patients to a social undertaking with the doctor-patient relationship as the core" (Yu et al.,

2015, p.9). Patient management is the core of maintaining stability. According to the notice issued by the NHC and the Central Political and Legal Committee in June 2023, clinicians should standardize the application of human-assisted reproductive technology to severely crack down on various illegal and criminal acts. The notice argues that improper management of fertility treatment and illegal services will seriously affect social order, security, and stability.

While most interviewees refrain from openly expressing their grievances toward formal institutions, unresolved frustration with clinicians and officials may escalate into instances of violent healthcare disturbance (*yi nao*) and petitions (*shang fang*).[5] The protest outside P Clinic serves as a stark illustration of how unresolved grievances can manifest into healthcare disturbance. The protesting couple's dissatisfaction with P Clinic's service, coupled with perceived inadequate redress by the clinic or the government, prompted their protest aimed at compelling P Clinic to address their demands. This protest not only tarnished the reputation and authority of P Clinic and the government but also underscored the deep-seated distrust of authority prevalent within society. In the following, I take healthcare disturbance as an example to elaborate on the three reasons why protests against formal institutions are sometimes unavoidable under the current policy framework.

First, existing administrative forms of mediation are widely considered to be expensive, complicated, unreliable, and unjust. For example, the couple who protested against P Clinic pointed out the difficulty in proving a clinic's responsibility for their child's illness within the confines of official medical malpractice mediation. The Regulations on Handling Medical Accidents (*yi liao shi gu chu li tiao li*) issued by the State Council in 2002 place the burden of proof on doctors and clinics in medical cases. Nevertheless, so long as they did not violate relevant laws and regulations through their negligence, it is easy for clinicians to claim that they are not responsible for accidents. Even if clinics are responsible, the compensation is low. Official H, for instance, explained how fines are only imposed on clinics for regulatory violations, sparing public hospitals due to the close personal relationships clinicians maintain with government officials. Consequently, patients find it challenging to seek

---

[5] To express their dissatisfaction about the service they receive in hospitals and to get compensation, patients and their family members cry in front of hospitals, displace funeral objects in front of hospitals or even attack doctors. People petition to lodge complaints against government officials. The petition system is vital for ordinary people who want to voice out their dissatisfaction since the government does not allow mass scale protests. Petition is not easy. Petitioners are often forced to go back home or even sent to psychiatric confinement by local officials. These local officials are worried that petition will negatively influence their career progress.

resolution through formal mediation institutions. Moreover, the government's approach to petitions involves a combination of concessions and repression, allowing protests while also taking measures to curb certain actions and prevent escalation (He and Qian, 2016). When the couple appealed to the MOH, the institution sent security guards to drive them away. As the woman (2016) put it, "Officials help each other." The couple was disappointed that the government did not protect their interests.

Second, although people can approach courts when formal governmental mediation cannot help, the legal procedures governing medical disputes are considered controversial. It is difficult for plaintiffs to demonstrate that a clinic is responsible for an accident. Courts usually rely on reviews undertaken by medical litigation boards. Indeed, the couple who protested at P Clinic told onlookers that when they turned to the Supreme Court, the court followed the decision of the litigation board and attributed only minor responsibility to P Clinic.

Third, ordinary people do not bring their issues to the attention of civil society organizations, and the practice of insurance companies covering medical accidents remains uncommon in China. Most social organizations are still led by the government. What is more, the government strictly monitors non-government organizations (NGOs), especially those focusing on rights. For example, the Mediation Committee operates independently and without government funding, yet it remains susceptible to government influence when resolving conflicts.

The couple protesting outside P Clinic explored multiple avenues for redress but were dissatisfied with both mediation outcomes and court rulings. This lack of effective channels for resolving issues formally encouraged them to engage in disruptive behavior as a means of expressing their anger. Indeed, scholars have noted that more and more disputes are being resolved outside the governmental or legal system. According to the Chinese Hospital Management Association, the total number of medical disputes has been rising by 22.9% annually since 2002, whereas only a small number of disputes are resolved by formal institutions (He and Qian, 2016). And the number of health-related court cases did not rise with the significant increase in medical disputes, even after the Tort Liability Law (*qin quan ze ren fa*) was enacted in 2010. In 2014, for instance, lawsuits only accounted for 17% of the total number of medical disputes reported in that year. This implies that a majority of disputes are resolved through informal ways, and many escalate to the point of violence. As sociologist Jiong Tu (2014) introduced, sometimes patients' family members hire professional protesters (*zhi ye yi nao zhe*) and display funerary objects and corpses in hospitals. Other Violence includes threatening doctors, damaging medical facilities, impeding the operation of hospitals, and even killing hospital personnel. Violence leveled at doctors has skyrocketed. MOH statistics show that "the total number of violent incidents targeting medical staff and hospitals have jumped sharply from 10,248 incidents in 2006 to 17,243 in 2010, growing 13.9% annually" (Feng et al., 2013,p.78). *The Lancet*, the world-famous medical journal, has published several articles on evaluating the risk of medical disputes faced by Chinese medical institutions and medical workers and the challenging environment for medical practice in China. Their titles include "A new generation of Chinese doctors who are facing a crisis (Jie, 2012)," "Which Future for Doctors in China? (An, 2013)," and "Violence against doctors in China (Xu, 2014)." These articles find that Chinese medical institutions have become a "dangerous place," "battlefield," or "fortress," and that doctors now work in a "high-risk profession."

At least, according to Dr. D, the couple protesting outside P Clinic had not received compensation from the clinic. Despite this, they persisted in their protest. Would their protest succeed eventually? Healthcare disturbance can be viewed as "weapons of the weak." Political scientist James C. Scott (2007) developed this notion in discussing similar tactics among peasants in a Malaysian village. When faced with exploitation, peasants did not organize public protests or revolutionary struggles. Instead, they turned to more subtle methods (such as gossiping and making jokes) to undermine landlords' authority. Scott argues that weapons of the weak are effective in societies where formal resolution is unavailable. Health disturbance, as a weapon of the weak, empowers them in their struggles against hospitals and government authorities. Unlike formal institutional channels, these strategies are more accessible, straightforward, and less costly. And unlike civil rights protests, they require minimal social mobilization. For instance, the couple outside P Clinic avoided confronting clinicians and officials directly. They chose indirect means, such as singing a song titled "Little Grass," to express their dissatisfaction. In vividly describing their son's misery, lyrics such as "I am not as fragrant as flowers nor as tall as trees. I am like a little blade of grass that no one knows" (The Woman, 2016) won people over by arousing their compassion. What is more, being emotional and crying loudly put doctors and officials in an awkward, humiliating position, threatening to damage their professional reputations.

Government officials often perceive medical disputes as akin to human rights movements, fearing they could undermine the ruling regime, a concept akin to the term "politics of uncertainty" developed by political scientist Andreas Schedler (2015). Politics of uncertainty means that autocracies do not know how secure their ruling is. Activists such as Koby mentioned the government's concerns about activism. For example, Koby explained why the government was cautious about the online egg freezing debate and feminism. She (2017) put it, "egg freezing aroused the debate about women's reproductive rights. Officials are sensitive about human rights movements. They are worried that these movements are connected with anti-Chinese government organizations such as *falungong*. These grassroots movements can challenge the authority of the government."[6] For Koby, such debates, which touch on reproductive rights and human rights principles, are viewed as potential challenges to the government's authority. Indeed, posts on Weibo during the egg freezing debate illustrate how these discussions can morph into critiques of the government's policies and mobilize individuals against governmental control, thereby threatening political stability. For example, one Weibo user criticized the restriction of single women's access to egg freezing violates the basic human rights principles in the Constitution. As the government promotes the Constitution as its fundamental ruling basis, the post challenged the government's rule by law. Some posts even mobilized users to fight against the government, threatening political stability.

Government officials in China often feel insecure about gatherings and demonstrations of any size. As Koby (2017) put it, "they are worried that these gatherings are connected with anti-Chinese government organizations such as *falungong*." "The anxiety comes from the history of the Communist Party," Koby (2017) told me. "The rise of the Communist Party was based on a mass movement" (Koby, 2017). For Koby, grassroots protests represent an existential threat to one-party rule, mirroring the Party's own ascent. Accordingly, healthcare disturbance often provokes government officials to bring the situation under control so as to stop protests from spreading. In turn, they put hospitals under pressure to resolve disputes at any cost. This way of coping with social unrest is called maintaining stability (*wei wen*). As Official Q (2017) put it, "The government does not encourage the public discussion of human rights. Since the emergence of the Tian'anmen Square Movement, maintaining stability overrides everything (*wen ding ya dao yi qie*)." Though most disputes can be resolved this way, legal scholar Benjamin L. Liebman (2013) argues that the government's obsession with stability trumps legal rules. For the couple, gathering outside P clinic and complaining about the courts' omission worked as a means of threatening social stability. They expected that the government would eventually facilitate the resolution of their complaint in order to maintain social stability. The way in which officials dealt with the couple protesting against P Clinic also reflected the perceived need to maintain social stability. Although the government was not directly involved in the couple's disputes with P Clinic, they sent the police to maintain order. The police did

---

[6] *Falunggong* is a persecuted spiritual practice in China.

not allow the couple to talk with other patients, thereby preventing the dissemination of dissenting opinions among patients.

I described how the government tightened social and political control by cracking down on dissents in Chapter 2, despite rhetoric promoting societal and economic openness. The government's response to disputes and social conflicts reflects a policy shift. The tightening of control represents a policy reversal from Chairman Deng's decentralized party power, indicating adaptation within the context of spiral modernization. Indeed Koby noted the government is increasingly cautious about gatherings and protests to uphold their rule. She told me that many feminist groups in China face the risk of being branded illegal and that the government controls their activities by monitoring their leaders. According to her (2017),

> Some feminists were asked to "drink a cup of tea" (*he cha*) in local police stations or even sent to prison under defiance and affray laws.[7] What do defiance and affray mean? The government simply makes up reasons, such as raising illegal funds or collusion with foreign forces so as to force those feminists to shut up. … organizations censor themselves in order not to be banned by the government.

The intimation tactics such as "drinking a cup of tea" at police stations or imprisonment are justified in the name of stability, leading organizations to self-censorship to avoid government reprisal, perpetuating a climate of information control, and suppression of dissent.

Summary

The chapter explained the rationale behind regulations prioritizing patient management in fertility treatment. This chapter first discussed another form of uncertainty associated with authorities: patients' doubts regarding treatment efficacy and single mothers' concerns about their children's household registration status. The uncertainty was derived from a marketized medical system, unbalanced medical resources, and officials' inaction following Chairman Deng's reforms. Then, it explored how ordinary people express their distrust of profit-driven, hectic, unfriendly clinics, corrupt public officials, and overly bureaucratic governmental processes through disruptive behavior such as protests outside clinics. These protests serve as "weapons of the weak," challenging authority legitimacy and generating far-reaching subversive

---

[7] Drinking a cup of tea is a common strategy that the Chinese police uses to threaten dissidents and activists.

dynamics within the realm of ARTs. Authorities saw such subversive energies as threats; to them, they took the form of instability and challenges to their rule. The regulations thus emphasize patient management in order to maintain social stability. The chapter also mentioned governmental efforts to tighten social control in response to conflicts, exemplified by crackdowns on feminist groups as a means of managing dissent.

This chapter delved into another instance of spiral modernization. Policymakers pondered over social conflicts and disputes stemming from economic and political reform during Deng's era. Hence, they proposed a policy reversal aimed at tightening social control. The next chapter will conclude the book by critically examining gendered power relations in Chinese ART regulations.

Chapter 6

Conclusion

The overall aim of this study was to understand policymakers' and clinicians' rationale behind the controversial ARTs regulations in China. I aimed to make sense of the diverse regulations, ideas, and practices surrounding ARTs by turning them into a window into contemporary Chinese society. Before I started the ethnography, I was doubtful about my research questions. According to my initial reading of the regulatory documents on ARTs, narratives of these regulations were so ambiguous and inconsistent that it can seem that Chinese policies are issued at random. I was concerned, therefore, that there might be no rationale behind the regulations on ARTs for me to find. My conversation with Dr. D was the first interview I conducted as part of my fieldwork. This comforted me, for she mentioned several of ARTs' cultural, social, and political implications and raised questions about Chinese modernization policies. Nevertheless, the interview also added to the complexity of the research, for I had never thought about the relationship between fertility treatment and modernization.

As my research deepened, it became evident that many participants were acutely aware of the profound social transformations unfolding in China over recent decades and their entanglement with reproductive technologies. Over the past 100 years, China has rapidly industrialized, transitioning from an agricultural to an industrial society. The impoverished, backward country of the late Qing dynasty has been dramatically transformed and now commands respect and awe around the world. In particular, Chairman Deng's modernization policies have led to developments in technology and the economy, as well as the opening up of Chinese society. However, these policies have brought challenges, and the government has reversed some of Chairman Deng's policies to address them. The mixed feelings inspired by ARTs reflect these dramatic social changes.

In Chapter 1, I introduced how the government's emphasis on technological innovation and population quality during the Deng era propelled the development of ARTs in China. At the same time, I showed how the ARTs regulations on medicalization, marital status, and doctor-patient relationships aroused controversies. I also discussed several dimensions of uncertainty in ARTs, which inform the twists and turns of the Chinese modernization path.

Drawing from Hegel's dialectics, I developed the theoretical concept of spiral modernization to refer to the reversals and continuities of Chinese modernization policies. As I traced in Chapter 2, from the late Qing dynasty to the People's Republic of China, Chinese political philosophy changed from traditional Chinese dialectics to Marx's dialectical materialism, with political leaders leveraging dialectics to drive societal transformations. Spiral modernization explains why modernization policies are periodically reversed at critical junctures, as detailed in the four spirals of the Chinese modernization path.

From Chapters 3 to 5, I analyzed how ARTs regulations in China aim to cope with various forms of uncertainty. I also explained how reproductive uncertainty surrounding ARTs sheds light on modernization concerns such as the abuse of technology, the decline of patriarchal norms, distrust of expertise, and social unrest. In Chapter 3, I found that ARTs practices were pervaded by the traditional Chinese belief in predetermination and lack of control from the initial moment of gamete fertilization to live birth. Thus, the clinicians in this study encouraged people to conceive naturally rather than spare no effort in pursuing fertility treatment. This explains why regulations limit ARTs in medical conditions. Doctors only practice ARTs when there are no other options for natural conception. The clinicians emphasized the traditional belief of uncontrollability in order not to exercise excessive human control over fertility issues. For them, the abuse of ARTs, abortions, and late childbearing represented challenges stemming from the technological innovation and population quality during the Deng era, exemplifying a logic of control.

In Chapter 4, I analyzed how allowing single women to use ARTs could lead to paternal uncertainty. In China, paternal uncertainty is rooted in both evolutionary psychology and traditional Confucianism. On the one hand, the clinicians I interviewed equated single women with virgin women. ARTs, they suggested, would damage single women's hymens and take their virginity. Single women's loss of virginity before marriage would make their future husbands doubt their chastity and the lineage of future children. On the other hand, in some types of fertility treatment, such as sperm donation, where genetic paternity is missing, marriage and husbands' consent have served as the basis for establishing a child's paternity in China. If single women use donated sperm to conceive children, paternity is unknown, as marriage and husbands' consent are absent in single motherhood. Hence, for clinicians and policymakers, the criteria for women's marital status is a mate-guarding strategy. They repackaged the concept of paternal uncertainty to address issues such as sexual openness and flexible kinship.

In Chapter 5, I described patients' uncertainty about the effectiveness of their treatment plans and single mothers' uncertainty about household registration procedures for their children whose fathers are absent. This uncertainty was derived from expensive healthcare costs, poor medical service, and ambiguous policies. Such uncertainty, if mishandled, could develop into subversive social unrest. The regulations on ARTs then urge clinicians to manage patients properly, such as developing communication and listening skills to maintain social stability. The chapter also elaborated on how the government managed social conflicts by tightening political control.

This book fills a critical research gap by providing solid research evidence to analyze the policymaking of ARTs in China. Existing studies often overlook the intricate social, cultural, and psychological factors that influence ARTs regulations and practices within the Chinese context. Few studies delve into the underlying rationales guiding the regulations on medicalization, marital status, and doctor-patient relationships. Moreover, published empirical studies on these topics are scarce, with most articles focusing on legal and ethical analyses. For example, although studies by Liu and Greenblatt (2012) and Vallejo et al. (2013) analyze age limits for egg freezing, they lack contextual depth and fail to analyze clinicians' underlying reasoning. Consequently, a dearth of understanding exists regarding the processes involved in formulating and implementing ARTs regulations. Thus, this book stands out as a pioneering study to explore the multifaceted social, cultural, and political dimensions of ARTs regulations in China. I made a distinctive and substantial contribution to the existing literature by moving beyond a strictly legalistic account of ARTs and offering a more overarching sociological analysis.

This book broadens the scope of current scholarly work on ARTs. One significant finding is Chinese clinicians' understanding of *Ming*, a transcendent force, in coping with failures of fertility treatment. According to them, ARTs, despite being advertised as a certain way of achieving fertilization, pregnancy, and healthy children, are, in fact, out of human control. Studies in other countries also notice institutions and individuals draw on metaphysical resources to respond to the uncertainty of fertility treatment. According to Bharadwaj (2003), Indian clinics place Hindu idols in their halls since Indian people believe the success or failure of fertility treatment is in the hands of god. Even in developed countries, the power of god in human reproduction does not fade away. For example, in *God's Laboratory: Assisted Reproduction in the Andes*, sociologist Elizabeth F. S. Roberts (2012) described that clinics place statues of the Virgin Mary, and clinicians pray to God before embryo transplantation. However, while previous studies focus primarily on individual experiences, the discussion on "*Ming*" among Chinese clinicians in this book provides unique insights into the intersection of traditional beliefs and modernization policies in China.

Moreover, this book reveals diverse ARTs practices and motivations in China. For example, during my fieldwork, I found married women freeze eggs when their husbands' sperm were not ready. I also found single women preferred egg freezing over embryo freezing despite the latter's higher success rates. While existing literature often emphasizes women's pursuit of egg freezing for personal reproductive autonomy, this study demonstrates that women in China also freeze eggs to ensure genetic relatedness between their children and their husbands (or future husbands).

This book also sheds light on the dynamics of interactions between clinicians and patients in the context of ARTs. While previous literature predominantly focuses on the psychological impacts of fertility treatment on patients (Newton et al., 1990; Cousineau and Domar, 2007) or their feedback on treatment experiences (Malin et al., 2001; Groh and Wagner, 2005; Dancet et al., 2010; Huppelschoten et al., 2013), little attention has been paid to how clinicians navigate conversations about fertility treatment, particularly when delivering bad news such as misdiagnosis and treatment failures. This book reveals that clinicians comforted patients through the traditional belief of *Ming*, attributing outcomes to a higher force beyond human control. This book also highlights that doctor-patient communication in ARTs practices in China was not always effective. Misunderstanding and poor service dented patient trust and clinician authority.

I have contributed to the existing literature on ARTs by illuminating the tensions between reproductive uncertainty surrounding ARTs and modern values such as rationality and liberalism. The uncertainty analyzed in this book challenges the modern worldview of risks. "From the 19th century, with the development of probability calculation, the concept of uncertainty became technical, closely dependent on the computability of phenomena" (Battistelli and Galantino, 2019, p.66). The notion of uncertainty was eventually reduced to specific, calculable risks that could be rationally managed. The perception of risks was then closely related to rationalization, control of nature, and human agency (Castel, 1991, 2003; Lupton, 1999). While uncertainty means uncontrollability, risks are viewed as the product of calculative-probabilistic calculation. In his book *Risk, Uncertainty and Profit*, Knight (1921) made a clear distinction between risk and uncertainty:

> Uncertainty must be taken in a sense radically distinct from the familiar notion of risk, from which it has never been properly separated. ... [I]t will appear that a measurable uncertainty, or proper risk ... is so far different from an unmeasurable one that it is not in effect an uncertainty at all. (p.19-20.)

For Knight, risks can be surmounted and rationalized by means of mathematical models.

Particularly since the 1970s, there has been growing interest in risk analysis (Burgess et al., 2016). With the development of modern society, policymakers have become increasingly anxious about the threats generated by modern society, such as climate change, natural disasters, terrorism, and market flux. Scholars like Luhmann (1995) and Beck (1992) have differentiated between risks originating from social systems and those stemming from external forces such as natural hazards.

The resurgence of faith and superstition among my interviewees challenges the assumption within risk analysis that uncertainty can be addressed through rational strategies. In *The Consequences of Modernity*, Giddens (1990) argues that new notions of risks and trust that replace pre-modern notions of fate are distinctly products of modern society. In other words, in modern society, the unanticipated exists as risks rather than a twist of fate or divine intervention. What I observed in my fieldwork makes for a stark contrast with Giddens' argument. Despite living in a modern society, many informants, including scientifically trained clinicians, maintain traditional beliefs centered around the concept of "*Ming*," which governs human life. This belief in fate underscores the persistence of uncertainty that cannot be reduced to probabilistic calculations.

In modern society, uncertainty has been overshadowed by the concept of calculable risks, granting individuals greater freedom in decision-making. ARTs, marketed as a rational and scientific means of controlling human reproduction, are challenged by inherent uncertainties. This questioning of human agency's omnipotence highlights the enduring influence of traditional philosophies and norms. The traditional belief in *Ming* reflects a recognition of human limitations, contrasting with the progressive, control-oriented model of agency associated with modernity. Hence, ARTs, when viewed through the lens of pre-modern logic, defy the conventional narrative of liberal, agentic modernity.

I also contribute to modernization literature. This book offers a fresh perspective on China's nuanced reversals of many of Chairman Deng's modernization policies. The tightening of ideological control, resurgence of Confucian ideas, and promotion of pro-natal social policies exemplify these reversals. The development of Chinese society indicates modernization does not irrevocably change society, separating us forever from our primitive, pre-modern ancestors. In examining the uncertainty surrounding ARTs within the specific socio-cultural context of contemporary China, I introduce the concept of spiral modernization, wherein policy continuities and reversals coexist.

Spiral modernization challenges several conventional sociological concepts. Firstly, it confounds the tidy dualism between tradition and modernization. Tradition is no longer the "other" against which modernity is defined, and modernity is no longer tradition's antithesis. Instead, the two systems mutually form one another. The reinvigoration of traditional beliefs among my interviewees, such as *Ming, Baoying*, and paternal uncertainty, reflects a complex interplay between tradition and modernity in contemporary Chinese society. Traditional values serve as valuable resources for addressing modern challenges. For instance, my interviewees emphasized the traditional notion of paternal uncertainty in response to liberal attitudes toward sex. Thus, tradition in the Chinese context is not merely an impediment to modernization but can also offer solutions to some of modernization's drawbacks.

Secondly, spiral modernization challenges the linear and progressive narrative of modernization. Concepts like technological innovation and population control, which were central to the modernization efforts during Deng's era, no longer fully capture the complexities of contemporary Chinese society. Instead, these policies have faced partial reversals as they encountered social challenges. Spiral modernization acknowledges the coexistence of continuities and reversals within the modernization process, highlighting the dynamic and nonlinear nature of societal change.

Now, I want to return to the question with which I opened this book: how do we understand ARTs regulations in China? Throughout the empirical chapters of this book, I endeavored to maintain impartiality and refrain from delving into ethical debates, such as whether medicalization compromises individuals' reproductive autonomy or whether ARTs should be equally accessible to single or diverse sexuality and gender (DSG) individuals as they are to cisgender heterosexual married couples. However, I do recognize the inherently gendered nature of ARTs regulations in China. For example, unlike egg freezing, national regulations do not explicitly require marriage for sperm freezing, and they do allow men to freeze sperm for non-medical purposes. Consequently, there hasn't been an establishment of egg banks in China. By contrast, according to the *Book*, "Up until 2012, The MOH identified 44 sperm banks and 126 clinics that provided artificial insemination with donated sperm in China. Two hundred fourteen clinics were licensed to provide artificial insemination with husbands' own sperm" (Yu 2015, p.5).

Policymakers and clinicians do not view these gendered policies as discriminatory against women; instead, they argue that these policies are designed to safeguard women's well-being. Many interviewees expressed concerns about the welfare of single mothers conceiving with donated sperm, believing that women may struggle to raise children alone. Therefore, they contend that restricting single motherhood does not impede women's reproductive rights but rather shields them from the potential conflicts between professional and family responsibilities. Similarly, the clinicians in this study claimed using ARTs to delay childbearing would harm women's own welfare. "Young women nowadays are too naïve," said Dr. D (2016c), "Who will take care of them when they become old, but their children are still young?" Dr. D argues that early childbearing could ultimately benefit women, as having children at a younger age would mean that their children would be able to care for them in their later years. Thus, for Dr. D, early childbearing is not detrimental to women's interests.

Many ideas raised by my interviewees, such as *Ming*, *Baoying*, paternal uncertainty, and social conflicts, may seem to justify gendered policies. However, I argue that these policies, ostensibly aimed at protecting women, actually serve to safeguard the interests of men while disregarding the needs of women. For instance, the regulations prohibit single women from accessing ARTs, and officials impose numerous barriers to their ability to conceive children. While it is argued that these measures promote stable family structures with husbands, they undeniably marginalize single mothers and their children in society. The underlying rationale behind such policies is to mitigate legal uncertainties surrounding paternity.

This book indicates many policy narratives are male-centered. I am aware that the *Book* mentions the term "unfair" when it describes single men's reproductive rights. Unfairness means men's reproductive rights are contingent upon women's cooperation. To be "fair," the government has enacted relatively lenient national regulations regarding sperm freezing. Following Jilin Province's decision to allow single women to conceive in 2002, there was considerable debate regarding single men's reproductive rights. Some legal scholars, such as Li (2003) and Zhang and Xu (2007), argue that restricting women's reproductive rights is necessary to protect men's reproductive autonomy. Others, like Zhang (2003), Peng (2004), Zhang (2005), and Cai and Liu (2011), advocate for legalizing surrogacy to safeguard single men's reproductive rights. These perspectives solely consider men's interests.

The book highlights norms experienced differently by men and women. My interviewees suggest that, unlike women, men do not view parenthood through the lens of *Ming*. They argue that while women experience menopause, men do not, making early marriage and childbearing societal norms for women. Women who deviate from these norms will be punished. Guilan discussed her husband's punishment. Her husband's sperm was unqualified on the day of gamete retrieval. However, she was subject to greater blame, as evidenced by her abortion experience.

Many policies discussed in this book are paternalistic. Policymakers and clinicians see themselves as custodians of societal norms. These norms are not only related to reproduction but also to women's social and institutional roles. Many of these norms are non-negotiable for women, resulting in their disempowerment. This book provides numerous examples of women being compelled to conform to norms dictated by *Ming*, medical standards, and political authorities. For instance, the pressure to maintain the appearance of traditional family structures led some single mothers to enter into convenience marriages, aligning with societal expectations and family planning policies. In doing so, they adhered to heterosexual norms, reinforcing societal ideals of family formation.

I also emphasize that narratives surrounding ARTs and ARTs regulations not only reflect gender inequality but also prioritize state interests. Disciplines of women's reproductive and non-reproductive lives serve to advance state policies. Women are mobilized to bear children only when deemed necessary by the state, with little consideration for their career advancement, educational pursuits, or personal autonomy. For instance, the government abandoned Late Marriage and Late Childbearing benefits to increase the birth rate. The officials and clinicians in this study argued it is a woman's responsibility to marry and conceive children in early life. They warned that women would get bad *Baoying* if they did not act in this normative way. As a result, the government reproduces a deeply entrenched form of ageism in China, disproportionately affecting women who face various forms of discrimination, particularly after the age of 35. Discriminatory practices extend to the workplace, where women are marginalized due to policies such as age-restricted civil service recruitment and salary cuts during maternity leave. Moreover, children born to single women encounter societal stigma due to government-defined household registration norms, reinforcing traditional heterosexual norms that bind paternity to various aspects of a child's life.

The government's handling of issues reflects its selective prioritization based on perceived state interests. For instance, before the controversy surrounding the first gene-edited babies in China surfaced, the government lauded the technology as emblematic of China's global technological prowess. Similarly, while the government expresses concerns about technology misuse, stringent measures to regulate widespread facial recognition technology were only implemented in 2024. Privacy rights in China have long been disregarded, with extensive surveillance tools used to manage crime and social unrest.

Policy-making in China is fluid and contextualized. This might explain why some regulations are puzzling and even conflicting, as they are drafted to address divergent needs and interpretations. While the government continues to view ARTs as integral to improving population quality, the discourse has evolved over time. Rather than aiming to produce superior births, ARTs are now primarily viewed as a means to address infertility, thereby enhancing population quality. According to the replies from the NHC to No.8569 Proposal from the 5th meeting of the 13th People's Congress, which requests increasing the number of fertility clinics, ARTs are of great importance in improving population quality (NHC, 2022). As the NHC elaborated, childlessness is the main factor that decreases population quality, and ARTs can address this factor.

It has been almost four years since I completed my PhD study. ARTs regulations remain largely unchanged. Marital status requirements for women seeking ARTs treatment persist, as evidenced by Teresa Xu's unsuccessful lawsuit against a Chinese hospital in 2019. However, there are indications of a shifting government stance. In August 2021, the NHC acknowledged the need for legal access to egg donation and storage, signaling a potential revision of management methods and technical specifications related to ARTs. Moreover, the Hunan branch of the NHC proposed allowing single women with medical indications to freeze their eggs, marking a departure from previous restrictions. Additionally, attitudes towards single mothers appear to be evolving, with the Sichuan provincial government granting them access to benefits previously reserved for married couples in 2023. These changes can be interpreted as the government's need for more childbirths. With the evolving social and political landscapes surrounding ARTs, how the government regulates ARTs needs continuous academic attention.

References

References for personal communication

Caifeng. (2016) Interview with the author, 13 September.

Dr. D. (2016a) Patients' consultation, 11 September.

Dr. D. (2016b) Patients' consultation, 12 September.

Dr. D. (2016c) Interview with the author, 2 July.

Dr. D. (2016d) Patient's consultation, 14 November.

Dr. L. (2016a) Interview with the author, 5 September.

Dr. L. (2016b) Patients' consultation, 6 September.

Dr. W. (2016) Interview with the author, 3 August.

Fuying. (2016) Interview with the author, 6 September.

Guilan. (2016) Interview with the author, 5 September.

Juzi. (2017). Interview with the author, 4 April.

Koby. (2017) Interview with the author, 3 March.

Lang. (2016) Interview with the author, 10 September.

Lao Bai. (2017) Interview with the author, 12 February.

Legislator Y. (2016) Interview with the author, 14 November.

Official H. (2017) Interview with the author, 15 September.

Official Q. (2017) Interview with the author, 9 March.

Palm reader. (2016) Casual talk with the author, 4 July.

Source anonymized. (2014) An article shared on P Clinic's WeChat platform about the biological clock.

Source anonymized. (2015) An article shared on P Clinic's WeChat platform to encourage early childbearing.

Source anonymized. (2016a) A patient's consultation with Dr. D, 19 September

Source anonymized. (2016b) A casual talk with a patient at P Clinic who attributed her infertility to having lost her virginity before marriage, July.23

Source anonymized. (2016c) A casual talk with a patient at P Clinic who complained about P Clinic's service, 12 September

Source anonymized. (2016d) A casual talk with a patient at P Clinic who complained about her clinician, 14 September.

Source anonymized. (2016e) Messages of a WeChat group, 14 September.

Source anonymized. (2016f) Messages of a WeChat group, 14 September.

The Women. (2016) The woman and her husband protested outside P Clinic. 2 July.

Tracy. (2016) Interview with the author. 23 August.

Rongfang. (2016) Interview with the author, 7 September.

Ruyi. (2016) Interview with the author, 21 July.

Weiwei. (2017) Interview with the author, 11 March.

Xiao Wang. (2017) Interview with the author, 4 January.
Yang. (2016) Interview with the author, 4 August.
Yanying. (2016) Interview with the author, 14 September.
Yuanhong. (2016) Interview with the author, 4 July.
Yuzhi. (2016) Interview with the author, 17 September.
Yuetong. (2016) Interview with the author, 4 July.
Yuetian. (2016) Interview with the author, 9 October.
Zhang. (2017) Interview with the author, 14 October.
Zhang Wen. (2017) Interview with the author. 15 January.
Zixuan. (2016) Interview with the author, 9 September.

Bibliography

A

ACOG. (2020) *Having a Baby After Age 35: How Aging Affects Fertility and Pregnancy.* Available at: https://www.acog.org/womens-health/faqs/having-a-baby-after-age-35-how-aging-affects-fertility-and-pregnancy

Aimagambetova, G., Issanov, A., Terzic, S., Bapayeva, G., Ukybassova, T., Baikoshkarova, S., Aldiyarova, A., Shauyen, F. and Terzic, M. (2020) The effect of psychological distress on IVF outcomes: Reality or speculations? *PLoS ONE*, 15(12). Available at: https://doi.org/10.1371/journal.pone.0242024

An, B. (2018) *Family Binds Nation, Its People, Xi Says.* Available at: http://www.chinadaily.com.cn/kindle/2018-02/22/content_35720770.htm

An, J. (2013) Which Future for Doctors in China? *The Lancet.* 382 (9896). pp. 936–37. Available at: https://doi.org/10.1016/s0140-6736(13)61928-5

Asian Development Bank. (2017) *Gender Equality and the Labor Market: Women, Work, and Migration in the People's Republic of China.* Available at: https://www.adb.org/publications/gender-equality-women-migration-prc

B

Bai, F., Wang, D.Y., Fan, Y.J., Qiu, J., Wang, L., Dai, Y. and Song, L. (2020) Assisted reproductive technology service availability, efficacy and safety in mainland China: 2016. *Human Reproduction (Oxford, England)*, 35(2), pp.446–452. Available at: https://doi.org/10.1093/humrep/dez245

Bai, L. (1998) Monetary Reward Versus the National Ideological Agenda: Career Choice among Chinese University Students. *Journal of Moral Education*, 27 (4), pp. 525–40. Available at: https://doi.org/10.1080/0305724980270406

Baird, D. T., Collins, J., Egozcue, J., Evers, L. H., Gianaroli, L., Leridon, H., Sunde, A., Templeton, A., Van Steirteghem, A., Cohen, J., Crosignani, P. G., Devroey, P., Diedrich, K., Fauser, B. C., Fraser, L., Glasier, A., Liebaers, I., Mautone, G., Penney, G., Tarlatzis, B., ESHRE Capri Workshop Group. (2005) Fertility and aging. *Human reproduction update*, 11(3), pp. 261‑276. Available at: https://doi.org/10.1093/humupd/dmi006

Battistelli, F. and Galantino, M.G. (2019) Dangers, risks and threats: An alternative conceptualization to the catch-all concept of risk. *Current Sociology*, 67(1), pp.64–78.

Baldwin, K., Lorraine, C., Nicky, H., Helene, M., and Stuart, L. (2014) Oocyte Cryopreservation for Social Reasons: Demographic Profile and Disposal Intentions of UK Users. *Reproductive BioMedicine Online*, 31 (2), pp. 239–45. Available at: https://doi.org/10.1016/j.rbmo.2015.04.010

Baldwin, K., Lorraine, C., Nicky, H., and Helene, M. (2019) Running out of Time: Exploring Women's Motivations for Social Egg Freezing. *Journal of Psychosomatic Obstetrics & Gynecology*, 40 (2), pp. 166–73. Available at: https://doi.org/10.1080/0167482x.2018.1460352

BBC Online Network. (1999) *China's Communist Revolution.* [online] Available at: http://news.bbc.co.uk/hi/english/static/special_report/1999/09/99/chi na_50/iron.htm

Beck, U. (1992) *Risk Society: Towards a New Modernity.* London: Sage Publications.

Beckert, J. (2016) *Uncertain Futures Imaginaries, Narratives, and Calculation in the Economy.* New York: Oxford University Press.

Bell, A.V. (2014) Diagnostic diversity: The role of social class in diagnostic experiences of infertility. *Sociology of Health & Illness*, 36(4), pp.516–530. Available at: https://doi.org/10.1111/1467-9566.12083

Bentham, J. and Charles, W. (2009) *The Limits of Jurisprudence Defined: Being Part Two of An Introduction to the Principles of Morals and Legislation.* Westport: Greenwood Press.

Bernstein, P. (1998) *Against the Gods: The Remarkable Story of Risk.* Hoboken: John Wiley & Sons.

Bernard, J. (1982) *The Future of Marriage.* New Haven: Yale University Press.

Bharadwaj, A. (2002) 'Conception Politics: Medical Egos, Media Spotlights, and the Contest over Test-Tube Firsts in India', in *Infertility Around the Globe: New Thinking on Childlessness, Gender, and Reproductive Technologies.* Berkeley: University of California Press.

Bharadwaj, A. (2003) Why adoption is not an option in India: the visibility of infertility, the secrecy of donor insemination, and other cultural complexities. *Social Science & Medicine*, 56(9), pp.1867–1880. Available at: https://doi.org/10.1016/s0277-9536(02)00210-1

Borovecki, A., Tozzo, P., Cerri, N., and Caenazzo, L. (2018) Social egg freezing under public health perspective: Just a medical reality or a women's right? An ethical case analysis. *Journal of Public Health Research.* Available at: https://doi.org/10.4081/jphr.2018.1484

Boulet, S.L., Kirby, R.S., Reefhuis, J., Zhang, Y., Sunderam, S., Cohen, B., Bernson, D., Copeland, G., Bailey, M.A., Jamieson, D.J., et al. (2016) Assisted Reproductive Technology and Birth Defects Among Liveborn Infants in Florida, Massachusetts, and Michigan, 2000–2010. *JAMA Pediatr,*170, e154934. Available at: 10.1001/jamapediatrics.2015.4934.

Braverman, A. (2002) Open-Door Sexuality. *University of Chicago Magazine.* 95 (1).

Branigan, T. (2014) *For Chinese women, unmarried motherhood remains the final taboo*. Available at: https://www.theguardian.com/world/2014/jan/20/china-unmarried-motherhood-remains-final-taboo

Britannica, (2022). *Taurt*. Available at: https://www.britannica.com/topic/Taurt

Brown, S.P. (2022) *Exploring the Association Between Female Infertility Stigma, Women's Cognitions, and Coping Responses Women's Cognitions, and Coping Responses*. Available at: https://digitalcommons.pcom.edu/cgi/viewcontent.cgi?article=1589&context=psychology_dissertations

Brokaw, C. (2014) *Ledgers of Merit and Demerit*. New Jersey: Princeton University Press.

Burckhardt, J. (1954) *The Civilization of the Renaissance in Italy*. Translated by S G C Middlemore. New York: Modern Library.

Burgess, A., Alemanno, A., and Jens, Zin. (2016) *Routledge handbook of risk studies*. New York: Routledge.

Buss, D.M., Larsen, R.J., Westen, D., and Semmelroth, J. (1992) Sex differences in jealousy: Evolution, physiology, and psychology. *Psychological Science*, 3(4), pp.251–256. Available at: https://doi.org/10.1111/j.1467-9280.1992.tb00038.x

C

Cai, S. and Liu, M. (2011) Dan shen nan xing sheng yu quan tan xi. *Journal of Hunan Police Academy*, 2011(4).

Cai, Y. (1984) *Cai Yuanpei Quanji (A Complete Collection of Cai Yuanpei's Works)*. Beijing: zhong hua shu ju.

Castel, R. (1991) From dangerousness to risk. In: *The Foucault Effect: Studies in Governmentality*. Hemel Hempstead: Harvester Wheatsheaf.

Castel, R. (2013) The Rise of Uncertainties. *Critical Horizons*, 17(2), pp.160–167.

Carroll, K. and Charlotte, K. (2017) Freezing for Love: Enacting 'Responsible' Reproductive Citizenship through Egg Freezing. *Culture, Health & Sexuality*, 20 (9), pp. 992–1005. Available at: https://doi.org/10.1080/13691058.2017.1404643

Cerebral Palsy Org. (2021) *Screens, Tests and Evaluations*. Available at: https://www.cerebralpalsy.org/about-cerebral-palsy/diagnosis/evaluations

Center for Disease Control. (2018) *Assisted Reproductive Technology (ART) | Reproductive Health | CDC*. Available at: https://www.cdc.gov/art/ivf-success-estimator/index.html

Charmaz, K. (2008) 'Constructionism and the Grounded Theory', in J.A. Holstein and J.F. Gubrium (ed.) *Handbook of Constructionist Research*. New York: The Guilford Press.

Charmaz, K. (2000) Grounded theory: Objectivist and constructivist methods. In Denzin, N., Lincoln, Y. (Eds.), *Handbook of qualitative research* (2nd ed., pp. 509–535). Thousand Oaks: Sage.

Chang, Kyung-Sup. (2010) The second modern condition? Compressed modernity as internalized reflexive cosmopolitization. *The British Journal of Sociology*, 61, pp. 444-64.

Chen, F. (1999) An Unfinished Battle in China: The Leftist Criticism of the Reform and the Third Thought Emancipation. *The China Quarterly* 1999, (158). pp. 447–67. Available at: https://doi.org/10.1017/s0305741000005853

Chen, S. (2005) *Human Being's Sex, Reproduction and Health.* Beijing: Peking University Press.

Chen, N. (1997) The Genesis of the Concept of Blind Fate in Ancient China. *Journal of Chinese Religions*, 25 (1), pp. 141–67. Available at: https://doi.org/10.1179/073776997805306977

Chen, G. and Cai, X. (2007) Clinical Application of Human Oocyte Cryopreservation. *Chinese Journal of Practical Gynecology and Obstetrics*, 23 (1).

Chen, P. (1981) *Rural Health and Birth Planning in China.* Research Triangle Park: International Fertility Research Program.

Chen, X. (2017) Zhong Guo Xian Dai Xing Wen Ti de Te Shu Xing Ji Qi Ren Lei Xue Fan Si. *Zhe Xue Yan Jiu,* 2016 (8).

Chen, A. (2009) Ren Gong Shou Jing de She Hui Ji Fa Lv Wen Ti Yan Jiu. *Law Space Internet Fortune,* 2009 (7).

CHICTR. (2018) *Zhong Guo Lin Chuang Shi Yan Zhu Ce Zhong Xin.* Available at: http://www.chictr.org.cn/showproj.aspx?proj=32758

ChinaDaily. (2018) *Family binds nation, its people, Xi says.* Available at: https://www.chinadaily.com.cn/a/201802/22/WS5a8dfb08a3106e7dcc13d42a.html

ChinaDaily. (2019) *National Science and Technology Ethics Committee.* Available at: https://www.chinadaily.com.cn/a/201907/31/WS5d40e064a310d83056401e10.html

China Media Project. (2022) *Two Establishes.* Available at: https://chinamediaproject.org/the_ccp_dictionary/two-establishes/

Choi, J. (2008) Work and family demands and life stress among Chinese employees: The mediating effect of work-family conflict. *The International Journal of Human Resource Management*, 19(5), pp.878–895.

Coleman, M. (2019) Women leaders in the workplace: perceptions of career barriers, facilitators and change. *Irish Educational Studies*, 39(2), pp.1–21. Available at: https://doi.org/10.1080/03323315.2019.1697952

Cook, S. and Dong, X. (2011) Harsh Choices: Chinese Women's Paid Work and Unpaid Care Responsibilities under Economic Reform. *Development and Change*, 42(4), pp.947–965.

Cousineau, T. M., & Domar, A. D. (2007) Psychological impact of infertility. *Best practice & research. Clinical obstetrics & gynaecology*, 21(2), 293–308. https://doi.org/10.1016/j.bpobgyn.2006.12.003

Crouch, C. (2004) *Post-democracy.* Malden: Polity.

D

Daemmrich, A. (2013) The Political Economy of Healthcare Reform in China: Negotiating Public and Private. *SpringerPlus*, 2 (1). Available at: https://doi.org/10.1186/2193-1801-2-448

Dancet, E.A.F., Van Empel, I.W.H., Rober, P., Nelen, W.L.D.M., Kremer, J.A.M., and D'Hooghe, T.M. (2011) Patient-centred infertility care: a qualitative study to listen to the patient's voice. *Human Reproduction*, 26(4), pp.827–833. Available at: https://doi.org/10.1093/humrep/der022.

Devroe, J., Peeraer, K., D'Hooghe, T.M., Boivin, J., Laenen, A., Vriens, J., and Dancet, E.A.F. (2022) Great expectations of IVF patients: the role of gender, dispositional optimism and shared IVF prognoses. *Human Reproduction*. Available at: https://doi.org/10.1093/humrep/deac038.

Davies, M.J., Moore, V.M., Willson, K.J., Van Essen, P., Priest, K., Scott, H., Haan, E.A., and Chan, A. (2012) Reproductive Technologies and the Risk of Birth Defects. *N. Engl. J. Med*, 366, pp. 1803. Available at: 10.1056/NEJMoa1008095.

Dikötter, F. (1998) *Imperfect Conceptions: Medical Knowledge, Birth Defects, and Eugenics in China*. New York: Columbia University Press.

Dirlik, A. (1975) The Ideological Foundations of the New Life Movement: A Study in Counterrevolution. *The Journal of Asian Studies*, 34 (4), pp. 945–80. Avaiilable at: https://doi.org/10.2307/2054509

Dirlik, A. (1997) 'Mao Zedong and Chinese Marxism,' in *Companion Encyclopedia of Asian Philosophy*. London; New York: Routledge.

Dong, G. (2008) Nv xing sheng yu quan ying you xian bao hu-cong an li fen xi de jiao du. *Legal System and Society*, 2008(21).

Dowd, N. (1997) *In Defense of Single-Parent Families*. New York: New York University Press.

E

Eisenstadt, S. (1984) *Modernization: protest and change*. Englewood Cliffs: Prentice-Hall.

Eisenstadt, S. (2003) *Comparative Civilizations and Multiple Modernities [A Collection of Essays]*. Leiden: Brill.

Eisenstadt, S.N. (1964) Social Change, Differentiation and Evolution. *American Sociological Review*, 29(3), pp.375. Available at: https://doi.org/10.2307/2091481

Ergin, R.N., Polat, A., Kars, B., Öztekin, D., Sofuoğlu, K., and Çalışkan, E. (2018) Social stigma and familial attitudes related to infertility. *Turkish Journal of Obstetrics and Gynecology*,15(1), pp.46–49. Available at: https://doi.org/10.4274/tjod.04307

F

Fan, D., Liu, L., and Xia, Q. (2017) Female alcohol consumption and fecundability: a systematic review and dose-response meta-analysis. *Sci Rep*, 7(13815).

Fei, X. (1992) *From the Soil, the Foundations of Chinese Society*. Berkeley, California: University Of California.

Feng, J., Li, Y., Han, C., Xu, L., and Duan, L. (2013) A Retrospective Analysis on 418 Medical Dispute. *Chinese Hospital Management*,33 (9).

Feng, Y. (2016) Dan shen nv xing sheng yu quan xing shi lu jing gou zao——jian ji ART shou duan de feng xian fang kong ping xi. *Journal of Ningbo Radio & TV University*, 2016 (3).

Foreign Ministry of the People's Republic of China (FMPRC). (2014) *President Xi's Speech at the College of Europe*. Available at: https://www.fmprc.gov.cn/mfa_eng/topics_665678/xjpzxcxdsjhaqhfbfwhlfgdgblshlhgjkezzzbomzb_666590/

Foster, D. and Ren, X. (2014) Work-family conflict and the commodification of women's employment in three Chinese airlines. *The International Journal of Human Resource Management*, 26(12), pp.1568–1585. Available at: https://repository.cardiffmet.ac.uk/bitstream/handle/10369/7681/Workfamily%20conflict%20and%20the%20commodification%20-%20Foster%20D.pdf?sequence=5&isAllowed=y

Franklin, S. (1997) *Embodied Progress: A Cultural Account of Assisted Conception*. London: Routledge.

Franklin, S. and Robert, C. (2006) *Born and Made: An Ethnography of Preimplantation Genetic Diagnosis*. Princeton: Princeton University Press.

Franklin, S. (2013) *Transforming Kinship*. Oxford: John Wiley & Sons, Ltd.

Frisby, D. (1988) *Walter Benjamin: Social Theory*. Cambridge: Cambridge University Press.

Fu, S. (1952) Xing Ming Gu Shun Bian Zheng. In *Fu Meng Zhen Xian Sheng Ji*. Taibei: Taiwan National University.

G

Gaines, J. (1991) *Contested Culture: The Image, the Voice, and the Law*. Chapel Hill: University of North Carolina Press.

Gameiro, S., Boivin, J., Peronace, L., and Verhaak, C.M. (2012) Why do patients discontinue fertility treatment? A systematic review of reasons and predictors of discontinuation in fertility treatment. *Human Reproduction Update*, 18(6), pp.652–669. Available at: https://doi.org/10.1093/humupd/dms031

Gareth, S J. (2019) 'European Socialism from the 1790s to the 1890s', in *The Cambridge History of Modern European Thought Volume 2, The Twentieth Century*. Cambridge: Cambridge University Press.

Gernet, J. (1982) *A History of Chinese Civilization*. Cambridge: Cambridge University Press.

Ginsburg, F. (1996) 'Mediating culture: Indigenous media, ethnographic film, and the production of identity,' in Deveraux. L and Hillman. R (ed.) *Fields of Vision*. Berkeley: University of California Press.

Ginsburg, F. (1989) *Contested Lives: The Abortion Debate in an American Community*. Berkeley: University of California Press.

Gilding, M. (2009) Paternity Uncertainty and Evolutionary Psychology: How a Seemingly Capricious Occurrence Fails to Follow Laws of Greater Generality. *Sociology*, 43 (1), pp.140–57. Available at: https://doi.org/10.1177/0038038508099102

Giddens, A. (1990) *The Consequences of Modernity*. Cambridge: Polity Press.

Glassman, R. (1975) Legitimacy and manufactured charisma. *Social Research,* 42(4), pp.615–636.

Goeking, K. (2019) China's One-Child Policy: Population Control and Its Unintended Consequences. *Women Leading Change: Case Studies on Women, Gender, and Feminism,* 4(2).

Government of the People's Republic of China. (2022) *Xi Jinping: Jia kuai jian she ke ji qiang guo, shi xian gao shui ping ke ji zi li zi qiang.* Available at: https://www.gov.cn/xinwen/2022-04/30/content_5688265.htm

Greil, A., McQuillan, J., and Slauson-Blevins, K. (2011) The Social Construction of Infertility. *Sociology Compass,* 5(8), pp.736–746. Available at: https://doi.org/10.1111/j.1751-9020.2011.00397.x

Greenhalgh, S. (2003) Science, Modernity, and the Making of China's One-Child Policy. *Population and Development Review,* 29 (2), pp.163–96. Available at: https://doi.org/10.1111/j.1728-4457.2003.00163.x.

Greenhalgh, S. and Winckler, E.A. (2005) *Governing China's population: from Leninist to neoliberal biopolitics.* Stanford: Stanford University Press.

Groh, CJ. and Wagner, C.(2005) The art of communicating ART results: an analysis of infertile couples' experience. *J Reprod Infant Psychol,* 23 (2005), pp. 333–346.

Gürtin, Z., Morgan, L., O'Rourke, D., Wang, J., and Ahuja, K.(2019a) For whom the egg thaws: insights from an analysis of 10 years of frozen egg thaw data from two UK clinics, 2008–2017. *Journal of Assisted Reproduction and Genetics,* 36(6), pp.1069-1080.

Gürtin, Z., Shah, T., Wang, J. and Ahuja, K., (2019b). Reconceiving egg freezing: insights from an analysis of 5 years of data from a UK clinic. *Reproductive BioMedicine Online,* 38(2), pp.272-282.

Gui, T. (2016) "Devalued" Daughters Versus "Appreciated" Sons: Gender Inequality in China's Parent-Organized Matchmaking Markets. *Journal of Family Issues,* 38(13), pp.1923–1948.

H

Harrell, S. and Santos, G. (2017) *Transforming Patriarchy: Chinese Families in the Twenty-First Century.* Seattle: University Of Washington Press.

Hao, Y. and Johnston, M. (2002) 'Corruption and the Future of Economic Reform in China,' in Arnold J. H and Michael J (ed.) *Political Corruption: Concepts and Contexts.* New Jersey: Transaction Publishers.

Haagen, E.C., Hermens, R.P., Nelen, W.L., Braat, D.D., Kremer, J.A., and Grol, R.P. (2008) Subfertile couples' negative experiences with intrauterine insemination care. *Fertility and Sterility,* 89(4), pp.809–816. Available at: https://doi.org/10.1016/j.fertnstert.2007.04.005

Handwerker, L. (2002) The Politics of Making Babies in Modern China. In *Infertility around the Globe: New Thinking on Childlessness, Gender, and Reproductive Technologies.* Berkeley: University Of California Press.

Hassan, M. and Killick, S. (2004) Negative lifestyle is associated with a significant reduction in fecundity. *Fertil Steril,* 81, pp.384–392.

He, A. and Qian, J. (2016) Explaining Medical Disputes in Chinese Public Hospitals: The Doctor-Patient Relationship and Its Implications for Health

Policy Reforms. *Health Economics, Policy and Law*, 11 (4), pp. 359–78. Available at: https://doi.org/10.1017/s1744133116000128

Hegel, G. (1996) *Lectures on the History of Philosophy, 1825-6*. Translated by Robert F Brown and J M Stewart. Oxford: Oxford University Press.

He, L. (1917) *Culture and Life*. Beijing: Shang wu yin shu guan.

He, K., Ho, H., and Zhang, Q. (2002) Urban Air Pollution in China: Current Status, Characteristics, and Progress. *Annual Review of Energy and the Environment*, 2002(27).

He, X. (2015) Qian xi dong luan bei hou de xiang guan fa lv wen ti. *Zhi Shi Jing Ji*, 2015(24).

HFEA. (2020) *Fertility treatment 2018: trends and figures*. Available at: https://www.hfea.gov.uk/about-us/publications/research-and-data/fertility-treatment-2018-trends-and-figures/

Hodes-Wertz, B., Druckenmiller, S., Meghan, S., and Nicole, N. (2013) What Do Reproductive-Age Women Who Undergo Oocyte Cryopreservation Think about the Process as a Means to Preserve Fertility? *Fertility and Sterility*, 100 (5), pp. 1343-1349. Available at: https://doi.org/10.1016/j.fertnstert.2013.07.201

Hornstein, M.D. (2016) Lifestyle and IVF Outcomes. *Reproductive Sciences*, 23(12), pp.1626–1629. Available at: https://doi.org/10.1177/1933719116667226

Huang, G. and Gove, M. (2011) Confucianism and Chinese Families: Values and Practices in Education. *International Journal of Humanities and Social Science*, 2 (3).

Huang, K. (1987) Face and Favor: The Chinese Power Game. *American Journal of Sociology*, 92(4), pp.944–974.

Huppelschoten, A.G., Johanna, W.M., Aarts, I.W.H., Cohlen, B.J., Jan A.M., Kremer., and Willianne, L.D.M. (2013) Feedback to professionals on patient-centered fertility care is insufficient for improvement: a mixed-method study. *Fertil Steril*, 99(5), pp.1419–1427. Available at: https://doi.org/10.1016/j.fertnstert.2012.12.024

Hunan Province Government. (2006) *Lu Guangxiu: Yong sheng zhi he gan xi bao ji shu zao fu ren lei*. Available at: http://www.hunan.gov.cn/hnyw/tpxwn/201212/t20121210_4849998.html

Huang, C. (2006) *Ren Lei Fu Zhu Sheng Zhi Ji Shu Ruo Gan Fa Lv Wen Ti Yan Jiu*. Master Thesis, Guangxi Normal University.

I

Ingraham, C. (2011) One is Not Born a Bride: How Weddings Regulate Sexuality. In: Seidman, Meeks and Fisher, eds., *The New Sexuality Studies: A Reader*. Routledge.

Inkeles, A. (1969) Making Men Modern: On the Causes and Consequences of Individual Change in Six Developing Countries. *American Journal of Sociology*, 75(2).

Inhorn, M. (2017) 'The Egg Freezing Revolution? Gender, Technology, and Fertility Preservation in the Twenty-First Century,' edited by R. S Buchmann and M. S. Kosslyn (ed.) *Emerging Trends in the Social and Behavioral Sciences.* Oxford: John Wiley & Sons.

Inhorn, M. (2013) Women, Consider Freezing Your Eggs. Available at: http://www.cnn.com/2013/04/09/opinion/inhorn-egg-freezing

Isaacson, J. (2018) *Freezing the Biological Clock: The Experience of Undergoing Social Egg Freezing for Delayed Childbearing.* Available at: https://open.library.ubc.ca/cIRcle/collections/ubctheses/24/items/1.0365943

J

Jacob, S. and Balen, A. (2018) Oocyte Freezing: Reproductive Panacea or False Hope of Family? *British Journal of Hospital Medicine,* 79 (4), pp.200–204. Available at: https://doi.org/10.12968/hmed.2018.79.4.200

Jiang, Q., Yang, S., Li, S., and Feldman, M. W. (2019) The decline in China's fertility level: a decomposition analysis. *J Biosoc Sci,* 51(6), pp. 785–98

Jiang, J. (1934) *Essentials of the New Life Movement.* New York: Columbia University.

Jiang, Z. (2000) Deng Xiao Ping Li Lun de Li Shi Di Wei He Zhi Dao Yi Yi. Available at: http://cpc.people.com.cn/GB/33839/34943/34983/2642170.html.

Jie, L. (2012) New Generations of Chinese Doctors Face Crisis. *The Lancet,* 379 (9829), pp.1878. Available at: https://doi.org/10.1016/s0140-6736(12)60774-0

K

Karayiannis, D., Kontogianni, M.D., Mendorou, C., Mastrominas, M., and Yiannakouris, N. (2018) Adherence to the Mediterranean diet and IVF success rate among non-obese women attempting fertility. *Human Reproduction,* 33(3), pp.494–502. Available at: https://doi.org/10.1093/humrep/dey003

Klawiter, M. (1990) Using Arendt and Heidegger to Consider Feminist Thinking on Women and Reproductive/ Infertility Technologies. *Hypatia,* 5 (3), pp.65–89. Available at: https://doi.org/10.1111/j.1527-2001.1990.tb00606.x

Klonoff-Cohen, H. (2005) Female and male lifestyle habits and IVF: what is known and unknown. *Human Reproduction Update,* 11(2), pp.180–204. Available at: https://doi.org/10.1093/humupd/dmh059

Knight, F. (1921) *Risk, Uncertainty And Profit.* Wilmington: Vernon Press.

L

Lao Z. (2010) *Dao De Jing.* Translated by Eno Robert. Available at: http://www.indiana.edu/~p374/Daodejing.pdf

Leite, R. C., Makuch, M. Y., Petta, C. A., and Morais, S. S. (2005) Women's satisfaction with physicians' communication skills during an infertility consultation. *Patient education and counseling,* 59(1), pp.38–45. https://doi.org/10.1016/j.pec.2004.09.006

Leow, R. (2014) China's health transitions. *The Lancet,* 384(9945), pp.738–739. Available at: https://doi.org/10.1016/s0140-6736(14)61427-6.

Leridon, H. (2005) The Biological Obstacles to Late Childbearing and the Limits of ART. *Ined-Inserm.*

Lerner, D. (1958) *The passing of traditional society: modernizing the Middle East*. With the assistance of Lucille W. Pevsner and an introduction by David Riesman. Glencoe: Free Press.

Li, Y., Xu, J., Wang, F., Wang, B., Liu, L., Hou, W., Fan, H., Tong, Y., Zhang, J., and Lu, Z. (2012) Overprescribing In China, Driven By Financial Incentives, Results In Very High Use Of Antibiotics, Injections, And Corticosteroids. *Health Affairs*, 31 (5), pp. 1075–82. Avaiilable at: https://doi.org/10.1377/hlthaff.2010.0965

Li, H. (2023) *Fighting on the Cultural Front: U.S.-China Relations in the Cold War*. New York: Columbia University Press.

Li, J. (2003) You du shen nv zi sheng yu quan yin fa de si kao. *Hebei Legal Studies*, 2003(3).

Li, L. (2016) Dong Luan Qian Xian Zhang Dian Zhi Shi. *Kan Shi Jie*, 2016 (11).

Li, L. (2016) Dong Luan Qian Xian Zhang Dian Zhi Shi. *Kan Shi Jie*, 2016(11).

Li, E. (2011) *How China Broke the West's Monopoly on Modernization*. Available at: http://www.csmonitor.com/Commentary/Global-Viewpoint/2011/0428/How-China-broke-the-West-s-monopoly-onmodernization.

Li, Z. (1981) *Historical Development of Esthetics*. Beijing: Cultural Relics Publishing House.

Lian, J. (2016) Dan shen nv xing leng dong luan zi fa lv wen ti tan jiu. *Bei Ji Guang*, 2016 (4).

Liang, J. (2019) *Xi stresses stronger cultural confidence*. Available at: http://www.xinhuanet.com/english/2019-03/04/c_137868756.htm [Accessed 14 Mar. 2020].

Liberman, R.F., Getz, K.D., Heinke, D., Luke, B., Stern, J.E., Declercq, E.R., Chen, X., Lin, A.E., and Anderka, M. (2017) Assisted Reproductive Technology and Birth Defects: Effects of Subfertility and Multiple Births. *Birth Defects Res*, 109, pp.1144–1153. Available at: 10.1002/bdr2.1055.

Liebman, B. (2013) Malpractice Mobs: Medical Dispute Resolution in China. *Columbia Review*, 181 (2013).

Linebarger, P. (1938) *Government In Republican China*. New York: McGraw Hill.

Lipset, S.M. (1959) Some Social Requisites of Democracy: Economic Development and Political Legitimacy. *The American Political Science Review*, 53(1), pp.69–105. Available at: http://www.jstor.org/stable/1951731?origin=JSTOR-pdf

Liu, K.E. and Greenblatt, E.M. (2012) Oocyte Cryopreservation in Canada: A Survey of Canadian ART Clinics. *Journal of Obstetrics and Gynaecology Canada*, 34(3), pp.250–256. Available at: https://doi.org/10.1016/s1701-2163(16)35185-4.

Liu, Y. (2007) China's Current Social Conflicts and Governance. In *7th International Conference on Social Network, Communication and Education (SNCE 2017)*.

Liu, H., Hong, L., and Dong, L. (2020) *Di Yi Sheng Ti Ku: Zhong Guo Shou Li Ren Gong Shou Jing Ying Er Dan Sheng*. Available at: https://www.chinastory.cn/PCzwsplby/video/20200106/10061000000450815782751699300068878_1.html

Liu, X. (1983) Lie Nu Zhuan Jiao Zhu. In *Si Bu Bei Yao*, edited by Duan Liang. Taibei: Zhong hua shu ju.

Luke, B., Brown, M.B., Wantman, E., Forestieri, N.E., Browne, M.L., Fisher, S.C., Yazdy, M.M., Ethen, M.K., Canfield, M.A., and Watkins, S. (2021) The Risk of Birth Defects with Conception by ART. *Hum. Reprod. Oxf. Engl,* 36, pp.116–129. Available at: 10.1093/humrep/deaa272

Luhmann, N. (1995) *Social Systems.* Stanford: Stanford University Press.

Lupton, D. (1999) *Risk.* London: Routledge.

Lu, P. (2008) Dan Shen Nv Xing Cai Yong Ren Gong Sheng Zhi Ji Shu Sheng Yu de Fa Lv Wen Ti Yan Jiu. *Legal System and Society,* 2008 (22).

Luo, R. (1993) *Xian Dai Hua Xin Lun: Shi Jie Yu Zhong Guo de Xian Dai Hua Jing Cheng.* Beijing: Commercial Press.

Lyotard, J. (1979) *The Postmodern Condition: a Report on Knowledge.* Minneapolis: University Of Minnesota Press.

M

Ma, T. (2006) Scientific Analysis of Buddhism and a Comparative Study of Buddhism and Science." *Frontiers of Philosophy in China,* 1 (4), pp. 594–629. Available at: https://doi.org/10.1007/s11466-006-0027-2

Ma, Y. (2017) *Da Hao Xin Xing Shi Xia Wei Wen Zhu Dong Zhang.* Available at: http://theory.people.com.cn/n1/2017/0113/c40531-29019766.html

MacLennan, A.H., Thompson, S.C., and Gecz, J. (2015) Cerebral Palsy. *Obstetric Anesthesia Digest,* 36(4), pp.185. Available at: https://doi.org/10.1097/01. aoa.0000504711.51311.45.

Mao, Z. (1937) On Contradiction. In *Selected Works of Mao Zedong.* Arlington, Virginia: Joint Publications Research Service.

Mao, Z. (1939) In Memory of Norman Bethune. In *Selected Works of Mao Zedong.* Beijing: Foreign Language Press.

Mao, Z. (2021) *Quotations from Mao Tse Tung — Chapter 21.*Available at: https://www.marxists.org/reference/archive/mao/works/red-book/ch21.htm

Mao, Z. (2019) *Quotations from Mao Tse Tung — Chapter 5.* Available at: https://www.marxists.org/reference/archive/mao/works/red-book/ch05.htm

Martin, L. (2010) Anticipating Infertility. *Gender & Society,* 24 (4), pp. 526–45. Available at: https://doi.org/10.1177/0891243210377172

Marx, K. (1872) Letter to the Zasulich. In *Marx and Engels Collected Works.*

Hekmatist. Available at: http://www.hekmatist.com/Marx%20Engles/Marx%20&%20Engels%20Collected%20Works%20Volume%2024_%20M%20-%20Karl%20Marx.pdf

Marcus, G.E. (1995) Ethnography in/of the World System: The Emergence of Multi-Sited Ethnography. *Annual Review of Anthropology,* 24(1), pp.95–117.

Martin, E. (1991) The Egg and the Sperm: How Science Has Constructed a Romance Based on Stereotypical Male-Female Roles. *Signs: Journal of Women in Culture and Society,* 16(3), pp.485–501.

Mate, S.E., McDonald, M., and Do, T. (2019) The barriers and enablers to career and leadership development. *International Journal of Organizational*

Analysis, 27(4), pp.857–874. Avaiilable at: https://doi.org/10.1108/ijoa-07-2018-1475

Malin, M., Hemminki, E., Räikkönen, O., Sihvo, S., and Perälä, M-L. (2001) What do women want? Women's experiences of infertility treatment. *Social Science & Medicine*, 53(1), pp.123–133. Available at: https://doi.org/10.1016/s0277-9536(00)00317-8

McCarthy, M. P. and Chiu, S. H. (2011) Differences in women's psychological well-being based on infertility treatment choice and outcome. *Journal of Midwifery & Women's Health*, 56(5), pp.475–480. Available at: https://doi.org/10.1111/j.1542-2011.2011.00047

Mohapatra, S. (2013) Using Egg Freezing for Non-Medical Reasons: Fertility Insurance or False Hope? - Legal, Ethical, and Policy Considerations. *SSRN Electronic Journal*, 382 (8). Available at: https://doi.org/10.2139/ssrn.2352111

Mussa, A., Molinatto, C., Cerrato, F., Palumbo, O., Carella, M., Baldassarre, G., Carli, D., Peris, C., Riccio, A., and Ferrero, G.B. (2017) Assisted Reproductive Techniques and Risk of Beckwith-Wiedemann Syndrome. *Pediatrics*, 140,e20164311. Available at: 10.1542/peds.2016-4311

Mullen, S.F., Rosenbaum, M., and Crister, J.K (2007)The Effect of Osmotic Stress on the Cell Volume, Metaphase II Spindle and Developmental Potential of in Vitro Matured Porcine Oocytes." *Cryobiology*, 54 (3), pp. 281–89. Available at: https://doi.org/10.1016/j.cryobiol.2007.03.005

N

National Bureau of Statistics. (1990) *China National Population Census 1990 - IPUMS | GHDx*. Available at: https://ghdx.healthdata.org/record/china-national-population-census-1990-ipums

National Bureau of Statistics. (2000) *China National Population Census 2000 - IPUMS | GHDx*. Available at: https://ghdx.healthdata.org/record/china-national-population-census-2000-ipums

National Bureau of Statistics. (2010) *China National Population Census 2010 - IPUMS | GHDx*. Available at: https://ghdx.healthdata.org/record/china-national-population-census-2010-ipums

National Bureau of Statistics. (2020) *China National Population Census 2020 - IPUMS | GHDx*. Available at: https://ghdx.healthdata.org/record/china-national-population-census-2020-ipums

National Health and Family Planning Commission. (2015) *Human Assisted Reproductive Technology Allocation Planning Guideline (2015 edition)* Available at: http://www.nhc.gov.cn/fys/s3582/201506/197803ad6e8041ba99fb58832787a128.shtml

National Bureau of Statistics. (2023) *guo jia tong ji ju: 2022 nian zhong guo chu sheng ren kou wan ren, chu sheng lv wei 6.77‰*. Available at: http://zw.china.com.cn/2023-03/01/content_85134736.html

National Health Commission. (2022) *Dui Shi San Jie Quan Guo Ren Da Wu Ci Hui Yi Di 8569 Hao Jian Yi De Da Fu*. Available at: http://www.nhc.gov.cn/wjw/jiany/202207/2700cba2c78a4d47a57921f16a3fc7b2.shtml

National People's Congress. (2021) *ren kou yu ji hua sheng yu fa xiu gai: wei cu jin ren kouchang qi jun heng fa zhan ti gong fa zhi bao zhang*. Available at: http://www.npc.gov.cn/c2/c30834/202109/t20210928_313795.html

National Health and Family Planning Commission (NHFPC). (2017) *Dui Shi Er Jie Quan Guo Ren Da Wu Ci Hui Yi Di 3395 Hao Jian Yi De Hui Fu*. Available at: http://www.nhc.gov.cn/wjw/jiany/201712/8a24174d2522466997c6942c65052ce5.shtml

Naples, N. (2001) A Member of the Funeral: An Introspective Ethnography. In *Queer Families, Queer Politics : Challenging Culture and the State*. New York: Columbia University Press.

Newton, C.R., Hearn, M.T., and Yuzpe, A.A. (1990) Psychological assessment and follow-up after in vitro fertilization: assessing the impact of failure. *Fertility and Sterility*, 54(5), pp.879–886. Available at: https://doi.org/10.1016/s0015-0282(16)53950-8

NICE. (2020) *Our principles | Who we are | About*. Available at: https://www.nice.org.uk/about/who-we-are/our-principles

Nichols, J. E., Crane, M. M., Higdon, H. L., Miller, P. B., and Boone, W. R. (2003) Extremes of body mass index reduce in vitro fertilization pregnancy rates. *Fertil Steril*, 79, pp.645–647.

NHC. (2022) *dui shi san jie quan guo ren da wu ci hui yi di hao jian yi de da fu*. Available at: http://www.nhc.gov.cn/wjw/jiany/202207/2700cba2c78a4d47a57921f16a3fc7b2.shtml

Nye, A. (1990) *Words of Power: A Feminist Reading of the History of Logic*. London: Routledge.

O

Olivius, C., Friden, B., Borg, G., and Bergh, C. (2004).Why do couples discontinue in vitro fertilization treatment? A cohort study. *Fertility and Sterility*, 81(2), pp.258–261. Available at: https://doi.org/10.1016/j.fertnstert.2003.06.029

Overmyer, D. L. (2008) Chinese Religious Traditions from 1900-2005: An Overview. In *Cambridge Companion to Modern Chinese Culture*. Cambridge: Cambridge University Press.

P

Pan, G. (1995) *Pan Guangdan's Collected Works*. Beijing: Peking University Press.

Pan, S. (2006) *Sex Revolution in China : Its Origin, Expressions and Evolution*. Gao Xiong Shi: Wan You.

Pan, S. (2017) *Sexuality among Chinese: 2000–2015*. Hong Kong: 1908 Limited

Parsons, T.(1951) *The Social System*.London: Routledge.

Parsons, T. (1964) Levels of Organization and the Mediation of Social Interaction. *Sociological Inquiry*, 34.

People's Congress. (2001) *Zhong Hua Ren Min Gong He Guo Ren Kou Yu Ji Hua Sheng Yu Fa*. https://faolex.fao.org/docs/pdf/chn205758.pdf

People's Daily. (1988) *1988 nian 3 yue 10 ri wo guo di yi ge shi guan ying er dan sheng*. Available at: http://pic.people.com.cn/GB/164277/171489/10252026. html

People's Daily. (2019) *Dai Ling Ren Min Chuang Zao Geng Jia Xing Fu Mei Man Sheng Huo*.Available at: https://baijiahao.baidu.com/s?id=1641151014830 695862&wfr=spider&for=pc

People. (2016) *Zhong Guo Gong Chan Dang Di Shi Er Ci Dai Biao Da Hui*. Available at: http://cpc.people.com.cn/GB/64162/64168/64565/index.html

Peng, X. (2004) Nan xing sheng yu quan wen ti tan tao. *Journal of Shanxi Politics and Law Institute for Administrators*, 2004 (2).

Platek, S. M. and Todd, K. S. (2006) *Female Infidelity and Paternal Uncertainty : Evolutionary Perspectives on Male Anti-Cuckoldry Tactics*. New York: Cambridge University Press.

Pletcher, K. (2015) *One-child Policy*. Available at: https://www.britannica.com/ topic/one-child-policy

Potts, M. and Roger, V. (1999) *Ever since Adam and Eve : The Evolution of Human Sexuality*. Cambridge: Cambridge University Press.

Pye, L. W. (1986) "Reassessing the Cultural Revolution." *The China Quarterly*, 108 (108), pp. 597–612. Available at: https://doi.org/10.1017/s03057410 00037085.

Q

Qin, Y. (1953) *Xiao Zichan Jieji de Sixiang Gaizao (The Thought Reform of the Petty Bourgeoisie)*. Shanghai: Shixi chubanshe.

R

Rabinow, P. (1996) *Essays on the Anthropology of Reason*. Princeton: Princeton University Press.

Rajkhowa, M., Mcconnell, A., and Thomas, G.E. (2005) Reasons for discontinuation of IVF treatment: a questionnaire study. *Human Reproduction*, 21(2), pp.358–363. Available at: https://doi.org/10.1093/ humrep/dei355.

Rainbow Society. (2016) *2016 Zhong Guo Dan Shen Nv Xing Sheng Yu Bao Gao*. Available at: http://www.rainbowun.org/uploadfile/2019/0219/201902191 12718415.pdf

Reischauer, E. (1965) The Dynastic Cycle. In *The Pattern of Chinese History: Cycles, Development, or Stagnation?* Boston: Heath and Company.

Rosenlee, L. and Hsiang, L. (2017) Ritual, Dependency Care and Confucian Political Authority. *International Communication of Chinese Culture*, 4 (4), pp.493–513. Available at: https://doi.org/10.1007/s40636-017-0107-0

Rouse, R. (1991) Mexican migration and the social space of postmodernity. *Diaspora*, 1, pp. 8-23.

Roberts, E.F.S. (2012) *God's laboratory: assisted reproduction in the Andes*. Berkeley: University Of California Press.

S

Sameroff, A. (2010) A Unified Theory of Development: A Dialectic Integration of Nature and Nurture. *Child Development*, 81 (1), pp.6–22. Available at: https://doi.org/10.1111/j.1467-8624.2009.01378.x

Schedler, A. (2015) *The politics of uncertainty: sustaining and subverting electoral authoritarianism*. New York: Oxford University Press.

Schuman, L., Witkin, G., Copperman, K., and Acosta-La Greca, M. (2011) Psychology of egg freezing patients: would they consider single motherhood? *Fertility and Sterility*, 96(3).

Scharping, T. (2013) *Birth Control in China 1949-2000 Population Policy and Demographic Development*. New York: Routledge.

Scott, J. C. (2007) *Weapons of the Weak : Everyday Forms of Peasant Resistance. Weapons of the Weak*. New Haven: Yale University Press.

Scott, R. B. and Richard, W. T. (1950) External Endometriosis- the Sourge of the Private Patient. *Obstetrical & Gynecological Survey*, 6 (2), p.277–79. Available at: https://doi.org/10.1097/00006254-195104000-00053

Scott, A. (2000) Risk Society or Angst Society? Two Views of Risk, Consciousness and Community. In *The Risk Society and Beyond: Critical Issues for Social Theory*, edited by Ulrich Beck, Barbara Adam, and Joost Loon. London: Sage

Shackelford, T.K., Buss, D.M., and Bennett, K. (2002) Forgiveness or breakup: Sex differences in responses to a partner's infidelity. *Cognition and Emotion*, 16(2), pp.299–307. Available at: https://doi.org/10.1080/02699930143000202

Sina. (2004) "*Qu Ge Luan Zi Dong Qi Shi Nian Ba Nian Hou Zai Dang Ma.*" Available at:http://news.sina.com.cn/c/2004-03-30/04302172409s.shtml

Sina. (2017) *Nv hai zui hao de jia zhuang shi zhen cao?* Available at: https://news.sina.cn/sh/2017-05-19/detail-ifyfkqiv6570513.d.html?oid=3Dsina&vt=4

Stanton, C., and Sussman, E. (2014) A Survey on Awareness and Interest Towards Proactive Egg Freezing among Women 25 - 35 Years Old. *Fertility and Sterility*, 101 (2), pp.34–35. Available at: https://doi.org/10.1016/j.fertnstert.2013.11.051

Statista. (2020) *China: acceptance of premarital sex among students by gender 2020*. Available at: https://www.statista.com/statistics/1257135/china-accep tance-of-premarital-sex-among-students-by-gender/

Steele, L. G. and Scott, M. L. (2013) The Pursuit of Happiness in China: Individualism, Collectivism, and Subjective Well-Being During China's Economic and Social Transformation. *Social Indicators Research*, 114 (2), pp. 441–51. Available at: https://doi.org/10.1007/s11205-012-0154-1

Sunderam, S., Kissin, D.M., Crawford, S.B., Folger, S.G., Jamieson, D.J., Warner, L., and Barfield, W.D. (2015) Assisted Reproductive Technology Surveillance — United States, 2013. *MMWR. Surveillance Summaries*, 64(11), pp.1–25. Available at: https://doi.org/10.15585/mmwr.ss6411a1

Supreme Court. (1991) *zui gao ren min fa yuan guan yu fu qi guan xi cun xu qi jian yi ren gong shou jing suo sheng zi nv de fa lv di wei de han*. Available at: http://www.law-lib.com/law/law_view.asp?id=7768

Sun, J. and Wang, X.(2010) Value differences between generations in China: a study in Shanghai. *Journal of Youth Studies*, 13(1), pp.65-81.

T

Taebi, M., Kariman, N., Montazeri, A., and Alavi Majd, H. (2021) Infertility Stigma: A Qualitative Study on Feelings and Experiences of Infertile Women. *International journal of fertility & sterility*, *15*(3), pp.189–196. Available at: https://doi.org/10.22074/IJFS.2021.139093.1039

The State Council of the People's Republic of China. (2016) *Guo Wu Yuan Ban Gong Ting Guan Yu Jie Jue Wu Hu Kou Ren Yuan Deng Ji De Wen Ti*. Available at: http://www.gov.cn/zhengce/content/2016-01/14/content_10595.htm

The State Council of the People's Republic of China. (2002) *She Hui Fu Yang Fei Zheng Shou Guan Li Ban Fa*. Available at: https://www.gov.cn/gongbao/content/2002/content_61699.htm

The Standing Committee of People's Congress. (2002) *The Policies on Population and Family Planning in Jilin Province*. Available at: http://www.34law.com/lawfg/law/1797/2419/law_464389384616.shtml#zx4

Tian, C. and Huang, Y. (2021) A comparative study of belief in Mazu and Guanyin in China. *The Journal of Humanities and Social Sciences*, 29(1).

Tian, C. (2005) *Chinese Dialectics : From Yijing to Marxism*. Lanham: Lexington Books.

Tian, K. (2019) Gai ge kai fang yi lai dang dui wo guo she hui zhu yao mao dun de ren shi. *Shandong she hui ke xue*, 2019(01).

Trivers, R. (1972) *Parental Investment and Sexual Selection*. Cambridge: Biological Laboratories.

Tu, J. (2014) Yinao: Protest and Violence in China's Medical Sector. *Berkeley Journal of Sociology*, 2014 (12). Available at: http://berkeleyjournal.org/2014/12/yinao-protest-and-violence-in-chinas-medical-sector/

U

UNESCO. (2019a) *School Enrollment, Secondary (Gross), Gender Parity Index (GPI) - China | Data. Data*. Available at: https://data.worldbank.org/indicator/SE.ENR.SECO.FM.ZS?locations=CN

UNESCO. (2019b) *School Enrollment, Tertiary (Gross), Gender Parity Index (GPI) - China | Data*. Available at: https://data.worldbank.org/indicator/SE.ENR.TERT.FM.ZS?locations=CN

V

Vallejo, V., Lee, J.A., Schuman, L., Witkin, G., Cervantes, E., Sandler, B., and Copperman, A.B. (2013) Social and psychological assessment of women undergoing elective oocyte cryopreservation: A 7-year analysis. *Open Journal of Obstetrics and Gynecology*, 03(01), pp.1–7. Available at: https://doi.org/10.4236/ojog.2013.31001

Van Empel, I.W.H., Dancet, E.A.F., Koolman, X.H.E., Nelen, W.L.D.M., Stolk, E.A., Sermeus, W., D'Hooghe, T.M., and Kremer, J.A.M. (2011) Physicians underestimate the importance of patient-centredness to patients: a discrete choice experiment in fertility care. *Human Reproduction*, 26(3), pp.584–593. Available at: https://doi.org/10.1093/humrep/deq389.

Vedom, J. and Cao, H. (2011) Health Care Access and Regional Disparities in China. *Espace populations sociétés*, 1(2011), pp.63–78. Available at: https://doi.org/10.4000/eps.4345.

W

Wallace, W. and Thomas, K. (2010) Human Ovarian Reserve from Conception to the Menopause. *Nature Precedings*, 5 (1). Available at: https://doi.org/10.1038/npre.2009.3179.1

Wang, L., Huang, X., and Liu, X. (2015) On Ethical and Legal Problems of Single Women' "Frozen Eggs". *Medicine and Jurisprudence*, 2015(6)

Wang, L. and Klugman, J. (2020) How women have fared in the labour market with China's rise as a global economic power. *Asia & the Pacific Policy Studies*, 7(1), pp.43–64. Available at: doi:https://doi.org/10.1002/app5.293

Wang, P. (2022) *China's population size and urbanization increased*. Available at: http://www.stats.gov.cn/tjsj/sjjd/202201/t20220118_1826538.html

Wang, JX., Davies, MJ., and Norman, RJ. (2002) Obesity increases the risk of spontaneous abortion during infertility treatment. *Obes Res*, 10, pp.551–554.

Wang, X. (2017) Hong Yang Chuan Tong Wen Hua Ying Li Zu Yu Jiao Yu. Available at: http://opinion.people.com.cn/n1/2017/0323/c1003-29162799.html

Wang, Y. (2019) When Tongzhi Marry: Experiments of Cooperative Marriage between Lalas and Gay Men in Urban China. *Feminist Studies*, 45(1), pp.13. Available at: https://doi.org/10.15767/feministstudies.45.1.0013

Wahlberg, A. (2016) The Birth and Routinization of IVF in China. *Reproductive Biomedicine & Society Online*, 2 (2016), pp.97–107. Available at: https://doi.org/10.1016/j.rbms.2016.09.002

Waldby, C. (2015) THE OOCYTE MARKET AND SOCIAL EGG FREEZING: From Scarcity to Singularity. *Journal of Cultural Economy*, 8 (3), pp. 275–91. Available at: https://doi.org/10.1080/17530350.2015.1039457

Wei, W., Wei, J., Rui, Y., Cui, W., Zhang, L., and Li, Z (2023) Analyzing the Trends and Causes of Birth Defects — Jinan City, Shandong Province, China, 2005–2022. *China CDC Weekly*, 5(44), pp. 978-983. Available at: 10.46234/ccdcw 2023.184

Wilson, M. and Daly, M. (1992) The Man Who Mistook His Wife for a Chattel. In *The Adapted Mind : Evolutionary Psychology and the Generation of Culture*. New York: Oxford University Press.

Woodhams, C., Lupton, B., and Xian, H. (2009) The persistence of gender discrimination in China – evidence from recruitment advertisements. *The International Journal of Human Resource Management*, 20(10), pp.2084–2109.

World Bank. (2024) *Labor force participation rate, female (% of female population ages 15-64) (modeled ILO estimate) - China | Data*. Available at: https://data.worldbank.org/indicator/SL.TLF.ACTI.FE.ZS?locations=CN

Wu, D. and Lam, T. P . (2016) "Underuse of Primary Care in China: The Scale, Causes, and Solutions." *The Journal of the American Board of Family Medicine*, 29 (2), pp.240–47. Available at: https://doi.org/10.3122/jabfm.2016.02.150159

Wu, B. and Zhong, X. (2014) Missing Men in College? Gender Difference in College Admission. *Journal of Tsinghua University (Philosophy and Social Sciences)*, 29 (2).

Wu, Z. (1997) *Ren Kou Ke Xue Ci Dian*. Sichuan: Southwestern University of Finance and Economics Publisher.

X

Xi, J. (2016) *Family Values, Family Education and Family Tradition.*Available at: http://en.npc.gov.cn.cdurl.cn/2021-12/27/c_693858.htm

Xi, J. (2021) *Lun Wenhua.* Available at: https://www.xuexi.cn/lgpage/detail/index.html?id=17255527699455210649&item_id=17255527699455210649

Xi, J. (2013) *Follow the Trend of the Times and Promote Peace and Development in the World.* Available at: http://toronto.china-consulate.gov.cn/eng/zgxw/201304/t20130419_7090386.htm

Xi, J. (2022) *Xi stresses upholding socialism with Chinese characteristics to build modern socialist country.* Available at: https://english.www.gov.cn/news/topnews/202207/28/content_WS62e1cc6fc6d02e533532e922.html

Xi, J. (2018) *Zai Bei Jing Da Xue Shi Sheng Zuo Tan Hui Shang de Jiang Hua.* Available at: http://www.xinhuanet.com/2018-05/03/c_1122774230.htm

Xi, J. (2017b) *Secure a decisive victory in building a moderately prosperous society in all respects and strive for the great success of socialism with Chinese characteristics for a new era.* Available at: http://www.xinhuanet.com/english/download/Xi_Jinping%27s_report_at_19th_CPC_National_Congress.pdf

Xi, J. (2014) *Qing Nian Yao Zi Jue Jian Xing She Hui Zhu Yi He Xin Jia Zhi Guan-Zai Bei Jing Da Xue Shi Sheng Zuo Tan Hui Shang de Jiang Hua.* Available at: http://www.xinhuanet.com/politics/2014-05/05/c_1110528066.htm

Xi, X. (2017a) Reasons for China's Changing Female Labor Force Participation Rate. In *7th International Conference on Education, Management, Information and Mechanical Engineering.* Amsterdam: Atlantis Press.

Xi, J. (2018) *zai bei jing da xue shi sheng zuo tan hui shang de jiang hua.* Available at: http://www.xinhuanet.com/2018-05/03/c_1122774230.htm

Xinhua. (2015) *Xi Jinping: Jian chi yun yong bian zheng wei wu zhu yi shi jie guan fang fa lun.* Available at: http://www.xinhuanet.com/politics/2015-01/24/c_1114116751.htm

Xinhua. (2016) *Ting Xi Da Da Tan Chuan Tong Wen Hua.* Available at: http://www.xinhuanet.com/politics/2016-01/31/c_1117948387.htm

Xinhua. (2018) *Xi Jingping: Zai Qing Zhu Gai Ge Kai Fang 40 Zhou Nian de Jiang Hua.* Available at: http://www.xinhuanet.com/politics/leaders/2018-12/18/c_1123872025.htm

Xinhua. (2023) *Xi stresses building Beautiful China, advancing modernization featuring human-nature harmony.* Available at: http://english.www.gov.cn/news/202307/19/content_WS64b69768c6d0868f4e8dde63.html

Xinhua. (2019) *Xi Presides over 9th Meeting of Central Committee for Deepening Overall Reform - Xinhua | English.*Available at: http://www.xinhuanet.com/english/2019-07/25/c_138254959.htm

Xiao, J. (2022) China Tells Women to 'Respect Family Values' in Revised Law. Available at: https://www.bloomberg.com/news/articles/2022-11-03/china-tells-women-to-respect-family-values-in-revised-law

Xiao, Z., Mehrotra, P., and Zimmerman, R. (2011) Sexual Revolution in China: Implications for Chinese Women and Society. *AIDS Care*, 23 (sup1), pp. 105–12. Available at: https://doi.org/10.1080/09540121.2010.532537

Xu, W. (2014) Violence against Doctors in China. *The Lancet*, 384 (9945), pp. 745. Available at: https://doi.org/10.1016/s0140-6736(14)61438-0.

Xu, H. (2014) Shou Li Leng Dong Luan Zi Shi Guan Ying Er Wu Yue Jiang Sheng. *Yi Xue Zong Heng* 2014 (1). Available at: www.docin.com/p-960986446.html.

Xue, Q. (2017) *Xi Jinping Yu Zhong Guo You Xiu Chuan Tong Wen Hua*. Available at: http://theory.people.com.cn/n1/2017/1221/c40531-29721761.html

Y

Yang, KS. and Ho, D.Y.F. (1988) The Role of Yuan in Chinese Social Life: A Conceptual and Empirical Analysis. In *Asian Contributions to Psychology*. New York ; London: Praeger.

Yang, R.(2011) Between Traditionalism and Modernity: Changing Values on Dating Behavior and Mate Selection Criteria. *International Review of Modern Sociology*, 37 (2).

Yang, F. and Pan, R. (2016) *Study on Israeli Egg Donation Law*. International Conference Health Law and Bioethics.

Yi, H., Grant, M., Zhang, L., Li, S., and Rozelle, S. (2015) Intended And Unintended Consequences Of China's Zero Markup Drug Policy. *Health Affairs*, 34 (8), pp.1391–98. Available at: https://doi.org/10.1377/hlthaff.2014.1114

Yeh, A. and Xu, J. (2009) Decoding Urban Land Governance: State Reconstruction in Contemporary Chinese Cities. *Urban Studies*, 46(3), pp.559–581.

Yu, X., Zhang, Y., Huang, Y., Feng, Y., and Li, S. (2015) *The Ethics and Management of ARTs*. Beijing: People's Health Publisher.

Yu, S. (1997). Special Overview: Political Enthusiasm Exists Side by Side with Political Indifference. *Chinese Education & Society*, 30 (3), pp.65–71. Available at: https://doi.org/10.2753/ced1061-1932300365

Z

Zarrow, P. (2006) *Creating Chinese Modernity : Knowledge and Everyday Life, 1900-1940*. New York: Peter Lang.

Zhang, L. and Ren, Y. (2016) Leng Dong Luan Zi de Lun Li Yu Fa Lv Wen Ti Tan Xi. *Heilongjiang Administrative Cadre College of Politics And Law*, 121 (4).

Zhang, Y.(2016) Analysis on Related Legal Problems of Single Women's Frozen Eggs. *Medical and Legal Studies*, 8(5).

Zhang, X. (1992) *Deng Xiao Ping Ke Ji Si Xiang Yan Jiu*. Liaoning: Liao Ning People's Press.

Zhang, M. (2014) *Gong He Zhong de Di Zhi*. Beijing: Contemporary China Publishing House.

Zhang, G. (2004) *She Hui Zhu Yi You Xi Fang Dao Dong Fang de Yan Jin.* Yunnan: Yunnan People's Press.

Zhang, S. (2010) Ru Shi Dao Bao Ying Bi Jiao Yan Jiu. *Journal of Baicheng Normal School,* 2010 (1).

Zhang, Y. (2005) How to Identify Parents of Children by Assisted Human Reproduction." *Law Forum,* 2005 (5).

Zhang, Z. and Xu, X. (2007) Sheng yu quan de xing bie chong tu yu nan xing sheng yu quan de shi xian. *Science of Law(Journal of Northwest University of Political Science and Law),* 2007(2)

Zhang, Y. (2005) Du shen zhe sheng yu quan tan xi. *Social Sciences Review,* 2005(2).

Zhang, Q. (2003) Zai yi sheng yu quan. *Public Administration & Law,* 2003 (7).

Zhang, K. and Beck, E. J. (1999) Changing Sexual Attitudes and Behaviour in China: Implications for the Spread of HIV and Other Sexually Transmitted Diseases. *AIDS Care,* 11 (5), pp. 581–89. Avaiilable at: https://doi.org/10.1080/09540129947730

Zhang, W. (1997) *Ideology and economic reform under Deng Xiaoping, 1978-1993.* London; New York: Kegan Paul International.

Zhang, W. (2012) *The China Wave: The Rise of a Civilizational State.* Hackensack: World Century Publication.

Zheng, Y.(1998) 'Comprehensive National Power: An Expression of China's New Nationalism,' in G. Wang and J. Wong (ed.) *China's Political Economy.* Singapore: World Scientific.

Zhou, S., Da, S., Guo, H., and Zhang, X. (2018) Work-Family Conflict and Mental Health Among Female Employees: A Sequential Mediation Model via Negative Affect and Perceived Stress. *Frontiers in Psychology,* 9(2018).

Zhou, K., Zhang, X., Ding, Y., Wang, D., Lu, Z., and Yu, M. (2015) Inequality Trends of Health Workforce in Different Stages of Medical System Reform (1985-2011) in China. *Human Resources for Health,* 13 (1). Available at: https://doi.org/10.1186/s12960-015-0089-0

Zhou, X. (2010) The Institutional Logic of Collusion among Local Governments in China. *Modern China,* 36(1), pp.47–78. Available at: https://doi.org/10.1177/0097700409347970

Zhu, S. (2003) "Federalism" in Contemporary China– A Reflection on the Allocation of Power between Central and Local Government. *Singapore Journal of International & Comparative Law,* (2003) 7, pp 1–14.

Index